EARLY NUMERACY: ASSESSMENT FOR TEACHING AND INTERVENTION

Box

EARLY NUMERACY: ASSESSMENT FOR
TEACHING AND INTERVENTION

EARLY NUMERACY: ASSESSMENT FOR TEACHING AND INTERVENTION

Robert J. Wright, Jim Martland
and
Ann K. Stafford

P·C·P
Paul Chapman
Publishing Ltd

To Monica and Jack.
To Wendy, Alison and Helen.
To Shannon.

———————————————

First published 2000
Reprinted 2001 (twice)

Paul Chapman Publishing Ltd
A SAGE Publications Company
6 Bonhill Street
London EC2A 4PU

SAGE Publications Inc
2455 Teller Road
Thousand Oaks, California 91320

SAGE Publications India Pvt Ltd
32, M-Block Market
Greater Kailash - I
New Delhi 110 048

British Library Cataloguing in Publication data
A catalogue record for this book is available from the British Library

ISBN 0-7619-6528-9
ISBN 0-7619-6529-7 (pbk)

Library of Congress catalog card number available

Typeset by Anneset, Weston-super-Mare
Printed and bound by Athenaeum Press, Gateshead

Contents

Contributors

Authors

Robert J. Wright

Dr Robert J. Wright holds the position of Professor in Mathematics Education at Southern Cross University in Australia and is an internationally recognized leader in understanding and assessing young children's numerical knowledge and strategies, publishing many articles and papers in this field. His work in the last ten years has included the development of the Mathematics Recovery Programme which focuses on providing specialist training for teachers to advance the numeracy levels of young children assessed as low attainers. In Australia, the UK, the USA and elsewhere, this programme has been implemented widely and applied extensively to classroom teaching and to average and able learners as well as low attainers.

Jim Martland

Jim Martland is Senior Fellow in the Department of Education at the University of Liverpool. Prior to his appointment as Director of Primary Initial Teacher Training he held headships of primary and middle schools. His principal area of interest is the teaching of mathematics at the primary phase, especially the identification of low attainment at Key Stage 1. He currently directs the Mathematics Recovery programme in the UK. His work is with local education authorities (LEAs) and the University's Department of Continuing Professional Development delivering courses on assessment and intervention in early numeracy.

Ann K. Stafford

Ann Stafford's academic background includes graduate study at Southern Cross University, Australia, graduate study at the University of Chicago and Clemson University in the USA, a Masters Degree from Duke University and undergraduate degree in Elementary Education and Mathematics from the University of North Carolina at Greensboro. Her professional expertise includes administrative roles for gifted and remedial students; mathematics supervision in the School District of Oconee County in South Carolina; teaching positions in Early Childhood and Middle School Mathematics and teaching and research positions at Clemson University.

Ann has received professional awards and grants for outstanding contributions to the region and state for mathematics and leadership. She received Teacher of the Year whilst at Walhalla Middle School. She has been the recipient of state grants for the implementation of an Early Childhood Gifted Programme, the Elementary Mathematics Specialist Programme, and annual grants for the implementation of the Mathematics Recovery Programme in Oconee County and the state of South Carolina. She currently directs the implementation of MR in the USA.

Contributors to Chapter 9:

Dr Joanne Mulligan

Dr Joanne Mulligan holds the position of Senior Lecturer in Mathematics Education at Macquarie University, Sydney, Australia. She is internationally recognized for her work on children's number learning. In particular her research on multiplication and division concepts has been implemented through publications and professional development. Over the past ten years her work has included contributions to the development of the Count Me In Too Professional Development Programme in New South Wales schools and a large-scale Australian research council project on children's imagery and number learning.

Peter Gould

Peter Gould is the Chief Education Officer in mathematics with the New South Wales Department of Education and Training. He has been instrumental in designing the Count Me In and Count Me In Too projects. His major interest is the effective use of research in the design and delivery of mathematics education.

Acknowledgements

This book is a culmination of several interrelated projects conducted during the 1990s, many of which come under the collective label of Mathematics Recovery. All these projects have involved one or more of the authors undertaking research, development and implementation in collaboration with teachers, schools and school systems. These projects have also received significant support from the participating schools and school systems. The authors wish to express their sincere gratitude to all of the teachers, students and project colleagues who have participated in and contributed to these projects. We wish to thank the following organizations for funding and supporting one or more projects that have provided a basis for writing this book: the government and Catholic school systems of the north coast region of New South Wales, Australia, and the Australian Research Council; the School District of Oconee County and the South Carolina State Department of Education in the USA; the Wigan MBC Coalfields and City Challenge Programmes, and Sefton and Salford Local Educational Authorities in the UK; and other school systems in Australia, the USA, the UK and elsewhere.

Preface

This book has as its major focus the comprehensive assessment of children's early numerical knowledge and strategies and their advancement. Practical and theoretical aspects of assessment are explained in detail. A major feature of the book is a learning framework in early number that is applied in analysing the results of assessment and planning for teaching. The book is particularly relevant to the assessment and teaching of children in the early years of school, that is, 4- to 9-year-olds, and to older children as well.

The book provides a comprehensive approach to assessing a range of aspects of early number knowledge. This includes children's counting strategies; their strategies for adding and subtracting; their knowledge of number word sequences and numerals; their ability to reason in terms of tens as well as ones; and their developing strategies for multiplication and division. The book describes several other significant aspects of children's early numerical knowledge such as the use of finger patterns, combining and partitioning small numbers, the role of spatial and temporal patterns, and the use of base-five as well as base-ten strategies.

The theory and methods underlying this approach have resulted from research projects conducted since the early 1980s, which had the goal of comprehensively assessing children's number knowledge and documenting its development over time. In the 1990s these methods have been learned and applied by thousands of teachers who have participated in a range of research and development projects conducted by the authors and colleagues, in Australia, the USA and the UK. This approach is new and distinctive, and embodies an extensive focus on teacher development.

The book is of interest to all who are concerned with finding ways to better understand and develop children's early numerical thinking. Teachers, teacher educators and researchers whose work relates to this field will all find much of interest and use in this book.

Preface

Introduction

The Need for Early Intervention

In the 1990s several research studies have focused on assessing the number knowledge of children in the early years of school (Aubrey, 1993; Wright, 1991b; 1994; Young-Loveridge, 1989; 1991). Some of these studies have assessed the knowledge of school entrants and some have documented children's progress by assessing the children several times within one school year or yearly for several years. Apparent from these studies is that there are significant differences in the numerical knowledge of children when they begin school. A study by Wright (1994) described the three-year difference in children's early number knowledge, that is some 4-year-olds have attained a level of number knowledge that others will not attain until they are 7 years old.

What these studies also show is that, by and large, these differences in number knowledge increase as the children progress through the early learning years and beyond. Thus children who are low-attaining in the early years tend to remain so throughout their schooling, and the knowledge gap between low-attaining children and average or able children tends to increase over the course of their years at school. What is a three-year difference in the early years of school becomes a seven-year difference for low-attaining children after about ten years of school. The notion of a seven-year difference was identified in the influential Cockcroft Report (Cockcroft, 1982) on school mathematics in the UK. What also seems to be the case is that, even in the early years of schooling, low-attaining children begin to develop strong negative attitudes to mathematics. It is reasonable to suggest that these negative attitudes result from a lack of understanding of school mathematics and rare experience of success in school mathematics.

In the 1990s, governments and school systems in several countries

1

focused increasing attention on the extent to which their schools teach mathematics well and how well their children achieve in mathematics. One aspect of this has been the close attention paid to the results of international comparisons of aspects of mathematics education such as student achievement, curriculum content and teaching methods. Most recently in the UK and Australia, for example, there has been a particular focus by governmental agencies in education on mathematics in the early years. Of particular interest has been the need for, and feasibility of, intervention programmes for low attainers in the early years. Early intervention is important because it provides an opportunity for educationally disadvantaged children before the gap between their knowledge and that of average and high-attaining children is too wide, and before they experience too much failure.

Development and Overview of Mathematics Recovery

The Mathematics Recovery (MR) Programme was developed as a systemic response to the problem of chronic failure in school mathematics. The programme involves: (1) identification of the lowest attainers at the first-grade level, that is the second year of school; and (2) provision of a programme of intensive, individualized and group teaching to these children in order to advance them to a level at which they are likely to learn successfully in a regular class.

The initial development of the Mathematics Recovery Programme was undertaken in the north-eastern region of New South Wales, Australia, from 1992 to 1995. This development was a nationally funded research project and was undertaken collaboratively with regional government and Catholic school systems. It involved 20 teachers in 18 schools and approximately 200 low-attaining first-grade students.

Key Features
The key features of MR are:

1. Intensive, individualized teaching of low-attaining 6–8 year old children by specialist teachers for teaching cycles of length 10 to 15 weeks.
2. An extensive professional development course to prepare the specialist teachers, and ongoing collegial and leader support for these teachers.
3. Use of a strong underpinning theory of young children's mathematical learning

4. Use of a learning framework to guide assessment and teaching.
5. Use of an especially developed instructional approach, and distinctive instructional activities and assessment procedures.

In MR teaching cycles children are taught 30 minutes daily, for four or five days per week.

Assessment in MR

Mathematics Recovery incorporates a distinctive approach to assessing young children's numerical knowledge and strategies. This method is interview based and involves presenting numerical tasks in order to determine the extent of the child's knowledge and the relative sophistication of the child's numerical strategies. The assessment results in a profile of the child's knowledge across several aspects of early number and additional information about the current numerical strategies used by the child. Thus MR assessment accords with a profiles-based approach to assessment, with the advantage that it provides much more detailed assessment information than that typically provided by profiles. The profiling aspect of the assessment is particularly useful for documenting children's progress over time, for example for the duration of the teaching cycle or over the course of a school year. The assessment also results in specific and detailed guidance for teaching via the Learning Framework in Number which is described later in this chapter.

MR Teaching

Mathematics Recovery teaching takes full account of the results of assessment and focuses simultaneously on a range of aspects in early number. In MR teaching sessions the child is presented with tasks that are genuine problems for them. The tasks are carefully chosen to elicit numerical thinking that is just beyond the limitations of the child's current knowledge. The teaching sessions typically involve the child in thinking hard and thinking reflectively about aspects of early number. The experience in MR is that teaching sessions of this kind are those most likely to result in significant advancement in the child's early numerical knowledge and strategies. Mathematics Recovery teachers are continually assessing children's progress during the teaching sessions through careful observation and review of videotapes of teaching sessions. Mathematics Recovery assessment and teaching are fully integrated. Thus assessment informs teaching and teaching provides additional assessment information. Planning for teaching involves the application of the Learning Framework in Number which provides crucial directionality for teaching and ensures that teaching is at the cutting edge of the child's current knowledge and strategies. Thus the Learning Framework in Number includes models of young children's numerical learning, which provide a sound basis for hypothesizing the likely new learning for students. Development of the Mathematics Recovery Programme also included the development of a set of guiding principles for teaching in the programme, and a working method for teaching, which takes account of the guiding principles.

Guiding Principles for MR Teaching

1. The teaching approach is enquiry based, that is, problem based. Children routinely are engaged in thinking hard to solve numerical problems that for them are quite challenging.
2. Teaching is informed by an initial, comprehensive assessment and ongoing assessment through teaching. The latter refers to the teacher's informed understanding of the child's current knowledge and problem-solving strategies, and continual revision of this understanding.
3. Teaching is focused just beyond the 'cutting edge' of the child's current knowledge.
4. Teachers exercise their professional judgement in selecting from a bank of instructional settings and tasks, and varying this selection on the basis of ongoing observations.
5. The teacher understands children's numerical strategies and deliberately engenders the development of more sophisticated strategies.
6. Teaching involves intensive, ongoing observation by the teacher and continual micro-adjusting or fine-tuning of teaching on the basis of her observation.
7. Teaching supports and builds on the child's intuitive, verbally based strategies and these are used as a basis for the development of written forms of arithmetic that accord with the child's verbally based strategies.
8. The teacher provides the child with sufficient time to solve a given problem. Consequently the child is frequently engaged in episodes that involve sustained thinking, reflection on her or his thinking and reflecting on the results of her or his thinking.
9. Children gain intrinsic satisfaction from their problem-solving, their realization that they are making progress and from the verification methods they develop.

Method for MR Teaching Sessions

The method for MR teaching sessions is described by Wright (1999, pp. 191–2) as follows:

In working with Mathematics Recovery teachers, the following steps are the method for the teaching sessions. First, the teacher must hypothesize about the child's current ways of thinking. This is informed by prior observations in a current or earlier teaching session or in an earlier assessment session, and may concern, for example, the child's current arithmetical strategies, facility with number words or numeral identification. Second, the teacher tests their current hypotheses by posing a task or asking a question and closely observing the child's response. Third, the teacher modifies his or her hypothesis on the basis of the child's response, and so the cycle continues. The teacher must also continually monitor the child's willingness to tackle problems and how comfortable or at ease the child seems to be. Through practice and reflection teachers can learn to adjust, in subtle but important ways, the pace, difficulty and degrees of variation and challenge when interacting with the child according to perceptions of the child's ease and satisfaction when responding to the instructional activities.

Teaching should be tailored as closely as possible to the initial and ongoing assessment, and should be at the 'cutting edge' of the child's knowledge. Activities should be genuine problems for the child and teachers must routinely make microadjustments to planned activities on the basis of the child's responses. The child should be continually challenged, with the teacher aiming to bring about re-organizations in the child's thinking. These re-organizations are shown by new and more sophisticated strategies. The teaching sessions are intended to be intensive. However, our observation is that for the vast majority of children the teaching and interview sessions are usually a very positive experience. Children seem to experience intrinsic satisfaction from thinking hard and solving problems and their enthusiasm for the sessions increases as the weeks progress. We also believe that individualized teaching is necessary to achieve the intensity that is required in the teaching sessions.

Children's learning

As a result of participating in teaching sessions, we have seen that important and positive changes in attitude to mathematics can occur as children develop a new sense of their ability to do mathematics and to rely more on their own resources. Children's reflection on their mathematical activity is an important aspect of the teaching sessions and it can play a crucial role in bringing about re-organizations of current strategies. Closely related to reflection is the importance of giving children extensive thinking time and avoiding temptation to speak when they are solving problems. A key aspect of the teaching approach is to provide ample opportunities for extensive periods of thinking hard about arithmetical problems. We believe that children in need of a recovery programme in mathematics are likely to have had too few opportunities to think hard about arithmetical problems, and to reflect on their thinking.

Extension of MR to the USA and England

One of the characteristics of the Mathematics Recovery Programme is its applicability to a multitude of situations and contexts. The extension of MR to the USA began in 1995 with its adoption by Oconee County in South Carolina. By 1999 MR had been taken up by North Carolina, Virginia, Maryland, Wyoming and the Bahamas.

The initial training has an emphasis on individual assessment interviews and teaching. However, when the MR teachers are qualified they implement the programme in a variety of ways within their own schools. The greatest impact is on one to one teaching but teachers also work with remedial groups and whole classes. With experience they also begin to apply the MR methods to different age groups.

Mathematics Recovery teachers and leaders have directed numerous workshops aimed at kindergarten through to 8-year olds. Where the project has been taken up MR teachers and leaders have formed networks that provide ongoing support and additional professional development. Mathematics Recovery conferences are held annually for administrators, teachers and leaders, and are increasingly gaining an international audience.

The principles of MR have also been incorporated into undergraduate- and graduate-level courses but it is at school district level where the biggest benefit is felt. As the districts embrace the National Council for the Teaching of Mathematics (NCTM) Standards the Mathematics Recovery Programme gives a direction to the assessment and subsequent teaching by increasing teachers' knowledge of how young children think and reason. The programme is consistent with the efforts the states and districts are making to provide children with the opportunities to develop mathematical power, a central theme of the NCTM Standards.

In England the funding for the introduction of the Mathematics Recovery Programme came from the Single Regeneration Budget (SRB) of Wigan Metropolitan Borough's Education Service. SRB allowed several projects to be established, including pre-school education, early years and parenting, reducing levels of non-attendance, and supporting pupils through the education system and into work.

The University of Liverpool's Department of Education was commissioned to research international early years intervention projects and recommended the adoption of the Mathematics Recovery Programme. The first cohort of teachers was selected from schools which had identified in their development plan the need to tackle underachievement in mathematics at Year 1. Following the successful training of the first cohort of Mathematics Recovery teachers, the group continued to train as MR leaders. The leadership training involved visits with US trainers and leaders, presentations at the annual MR conference and visits to schools both in the USA and in England. In 1997 MR coverage extended to the Metropolitan Borough of Sefton. This was particularly significant because Sefton Metropolitan Borough Council clearly saw Mathematics Recovery complementing the work of the National Numeracy Project which was beginning to come on stream. Thirty-six teachers from 14 schools undertook the courses. The key idea was to establish learning teams within a school, typically these included the Mathematics Co-ordinator, the Year 1 teacher and either the Special Needs Co-ordinator or Classroom Assistant. The advent of a learning team has still to be evaluated as an In-service development, but early reports indicate that it is a very positive agent for change both for the school and for the personnel involved. By 1999 over 100 teachers in Merseyside had qualified in MR. Authorities using MR report that the National Numeracy Strategy gives a broad brush approach to raising attainment but that Mathematics Recovery provides a necessary, in-depth assessment tool and intervention course for the early years.

Count Me In Too – a Systemic, Classroom-Based Project Adapting the Key Aspects of Mathematics Recovery

Count Me In Too (CMIT) is an innovative project in early mathematics and is being undertaken in the government (public) school system in the state of New South Wales in Australia. The goal of CMIT is to improve student learning outcomes in early numeracy, through the professional development of teachers. The main focus of CMIT is the development of teachers' understanding of children's strategies in early number and how teachers can help children to develop more advanced numerical strategies. By the end of 1998, CMIT had been implemented in approximately 600 schools across the state. The development of CMIT involved adaptation of key aspects of the theory and methods of MR including:

- the guiding framework (Learning Framework in Number);
- the approach to assessment, and the assessment tasks;
- the underlying theory of early numerical learning;
- the guiding principles for teaching; and
- approaches to teacher professional development.

According to an independent evaluation of CMIT in its pilot year, the project was highly successful in terms of teacher professional development and student learning (Bobis, 1996). This is described in more detail in Appendix 1. On the basis of evaluations of each phase of the project it is being implemented as widely as possible in the school system and large numbers of schools are choosing to commit to its implementation. The success of CMIT and the high regard in which it is held by educational administrators, principals and teachers provide strong evidence that MR is readily adaptable to classroom teaching and to average and high attainers as well as low attainers.

In each of the years since its inception, the Mathematics Recovery Programme has significantly influenced general classroom teaching of mathematics and many of the participating schools have successfully applied MR theory and techniques to classroom mathematics. This influence has been particularly significant in schools where the MR teacher has a leadership role and where the programme is well supported in the school. These applications of MR to classroom teaching typically have occurred at the level of the individual school. Count Me In Too, by way of contrast, is a large-scale and systemic initiative. Considered together, these applications of MR theory and techniques to classroom teaching provide compelling evidence of the suitability of this approach to the teaching of number in the early years of school.

1999 saw the trial of CMIT by 90 teachers in New Zealand primary schools. CMIT has been adopted by the NSW Department of Education and Training as the equivalent of their National

Numeracy Strategy and will implement training for all schools (approximately 1,800) between 2000 and 2003.

The Structure of the Book

In this introduction we have indicated that change can be made, and that low attainment can be challenged and raised. Our task is to enable you, the reader, to have access to the full programme. Chapter 1 presents the origins of the Mathematics Recovery Programme and its development in Australia. It describes the extension of Mathematics Recovery to school systems in the USA and the UK, and an application of MR to classroom teaching. Chapter 2 provides a detailed description of the Learning Framework in Number which is common to all of these programmes.

Chapter 3 introduces the reader to the distinctive assessment process used in MR. This includes a discussion of general features of the assessment process, descriptions of the two Assessment Schedules and the various kinds of assessment tasks. The relevance of the tasks to the five models of early numerical development in Strands A and B of the Learning Framework in Number are explained. This chapter also includes as its final section detailed descriptions of a range of exemplary tasks which have relevance for both assessment and instruction in the programme. Children's early numerical strategies are also described and linked to these tasks.

In Chapter 4, the origin and background of the Stages of Early Arithmetical Learning (SEAL) are explained. This includes an introduction to the particular sense in which the term 'counting' is used in SEAL, explanations of the terms 'stages' and 'levels', and a discussion of the means by which children's numerical strategies may be observed. This is followed by a detailed description of each of the stages. Included in these descriptions are two examples of children's problem-solving activity relevant to the stage. These examples take the form of video excerpts, that is objective descriptions of the child's problem-solving activity. Each video excerpt is followed by a discussion of the problem-solving activity portrayed in the excerpt.

Analysis of MR assessment involves a good deal of learning on the part of teachers. This learning is best undertaken through practice, reflection and discussion, and Chapter 5 introduces the reader to this process. Twelve scenarios of children's problem-solving activity in early number are presented. These scenarios are based on actual assessments by MR teachers, and focus specifically on additive and subtractive tasks.

The exercise for the reader is to study each scenario carefully in order to determine the child's stage of development in terms of the SEAL model. This exercise serves several purposes. As well as providing important practice for the reader in analysing children's problem-solving activity, it provides insights into the ways in which teachers present tasks and interact with children during MR assessment, and exemplifies the diverse ways children respond to the assessment tasks.

Readers should bear in mind that MR assessment aims to determine the most advanced strategy available to the child. This is equally important in the administration of the assessment interview and its analysis. The child's use of this strategy should be spontaneous, that is, unassisted either directly or indirectly by the teacher. As a general rule the child should use the strategy in solving several tasks, rather than only the introductory task for example. Each of the twelve scenarios in this chapter has been selected because, in the view of the authors, it provides a reasonably clear-cut example of children's problem-solving at a given stage. Readers should aim to carefully identify each strategy used by the child and then determine the most advanced strategy available to the child. Each scenario is explained in detail and the particular stage is identified. Chapter 6 includes the specific instructions required to prepare for and administer the assessment interview and Chapter 7 sets out the directions for coding and analysing the assessment interview.

Working with teachers on the development of MR involved taking a problem-based approach to teachers' learning, and issues concerning the programme arose almost on a daily basis. The problem-based approach involved discussing issues in weekly teachers' meetings, suggesting appropriate courses of action and seeking feedback through observation and further discussion. Discussion of issues included reviewing current practice and research. Participating teachers undertook action research projects that aimed to illuminate key issues. Chapter 8 provides an overview of many of these issues.

The final chapter extends the work of MR by incorporating the latest research into the operations of multiplication and division. It has been written by Robert J. Wright, Joanne Mulligan from the School of Education, Macquarie University and Peter Gould from the New South Wales Department of Education and Training. The chapter includes:

1. an overview of the development of children's early multiplication and division knowledge and strategies;

2. an associated model consisting of five levels;
3. for each level, an explanation and an illustration in the form of a protocol of a child's solutions of multiplicative or divisional tasks;
4. an assessment schedule for early multiplication and division knowledge and strategies;
5. summary guidelines for determining levels of early multiplication and division knowledge;
6. five scenarios for which the reader is challenged to identify the child's level and solutions and explanations for the scenarios; and
7. exemplary instructional tasks for early multiplication and division.

Appendix 1 reports the outcomes of two implementations of the MR Programme – in Australia, in 1994, and in the USA, in 1995–96 – and outcomes of an evaluation of the CMIT project in Australia, in 1996. The reports relating to MR focus on the progress of participating children and illustrate the levels of student progress that can be expected in an implementation of MR. These reports also demonstrate how the LFIN is used to document progress of relatively large numbers of children over an extended period such as the school year.

1

Children, Numeracy and Mathematics Recovery

We would like you to meet three young children. Judy is Australian and attends school in New South Wales, Denise lives in the North West of England and Michael is from South Carolina in the USA. Their classrooms are thousands of miles apart, in opposite hemispheres and in different time zones. Though they receive schooling under different educational administrations, Judy, Denise and Michael share several features in common. First, they are approximately the same age being between 6 and 7 years. Secondly, at the time of the interviews all three have been in school for almost a year and a half. They are regular attenders and well adjusted to school. However, they also share a problem. They are all experiencing difficulty with basic numeracy and already they are falling behind the expected performance level of their year group.

Judy and Denise's teachers have assessed them informally in mathematical attainment and placed them in the bottom 10 to 25 per cent bracket within their year group. This does not qualify Judy nor Denise for additional attention or support. Michael, however, has been assessed as learning disabled based upon his psychological profile at the end of kindergarten, but is not yet receiving help.

We know there is ample evidence (Aubrey, 1993; Wright, 1991b; 1994; Young-Loveridge, 1989; 1991) to show that there are significant differences in the numerical knowledge of children when they begin school and that these differences increase as they progress through school. In other words, children who are low attainers at the beginning of schooling tend to remain so, and the gap between them and the average to high attainers tends to increase. Thus the question arises as to what will happen to these children if they do not receive additional support in numeracy other than that given by the class teacher as part of their normal duties? Further, since the vast majority of primary and elementary teachers are not specialist teachers of mathematics one might extend the question to ask whether the teachers are in a position to remediate the children's problems even

12

if they know what they are. Since neither Judy, Denise nor Michael are disruptive, rather classified as 'co-operative', there is a strong possibility that their difficulties may be overlooked. Let us look at the actual attainment of each child in turn and, though they are in different school systems, see if they experience common difficulties in numeracy lessons.

Judy

Judy has completed one and a half year's schooling. Her teacher assessed her knowledge of the number word sequence, the ability to name numerals, and strategies for solving addition and subtraction involving two small collections of counters both of which were covered from view.

Judy showed she had a sound knowledge of the number word sequence in the range of one to ten. She could 'count' from one to ten and backwards from ten to one. She could also say the number before or after any number word in the range one to ten. However, she was not able to do this for the numbers in the teens or twenties. When numeral cards were shown to Judy she was able to identify the numerals in the range one to twenty but was not able to name many beyond twenty.

Judy was given two verbal addition tasks, 5 + 4 and 8 + 3. First she was presented with five red counters as a group, which were covered, and then four green counters which were placed under a separate screen. She was asked how many counters were there altogether. She successfully solved these tasks but it is revealing to consider the strategy she used in doing so. She invariably counted from one using her fingers or making pointing actions over the screened collections. Her strategy could be described as counting one of the screened collections from one and then continuing her count to include the other screened collection. 'One, two, three, four, five . . . six, seven, eight, nine . . . Nine!'

Judy demonstrates that she possesses one-to-one correspondence and has good counting skills but these are limited to the range one to ten. She identifies numerals up to twenty. She understands the operation of addition but not subtraction. It is important to note that her current number knowledge does not include number facts to ten. She uses a strategy of counting from one to solve additive tasks. Mathematically this is a low level strategy. Given that she has difficulty with counting in the teens her strategy is likely to fail her when larger quantities are introduced such as 9 + 6 for example.

Denise

Denise was 7 years and 1 month at the time of assessment and had been in school for four terms. She could say the number words up to 27 but she had difficulty when saying the number that came after a number when it was above twelve. She also had a lack of fluency when crossing the decade number twenty. Her counting backwards skills were limited to saying the words from ten. When she was asked to start at fifteen and count backwards she said '15, 51, 52, 53'. She could say the number word that comes before a number but only if the number was less than ten. When asked to produce the number before a certain number between ten and twenty she always gave the number one more than, even when the task was repeated. For example, she would respond 'eighteen' when asked for the number before 17 and 'twenty-one' for 20.

Her numeral identification skills were limited to numbers less than ten. She said 'fourteen' for 47, 'fifty-five' for 15 and 'thirty-three' for 13. When Denise was given the same addition problem with the screened counters as Judy, that is 5 + 4, her strategy was to guess 'seven'. The task was re-presented and this time she stated 'six'. Other than guessing Denise did not have a strategy for solving the addition tasks. The teacher reduced the complexity of the problem by showing her five counters which were then placed under a screen. Two more counters of a different colour were displayed alongside but this time they were not covered. She was asked 'How many are there alto-gether?' The teacher indicated the total collection by a circular motion of the hand. Denise failed to answer 5 + 2, 4 + 4 and 7 + 5 correctly. The level of the tasks was reduced even further by checking if Denise's had one-to-one correspondence. First a linear collection of 13 coun-ters was presented and, secondly, one of 18 counters. Denise suc-cessfully demonstrated that she had good one-to-one correspondence in this range.

Michael

Michael could count forwards up to 29 but halted at twenty. He could not say the number that came after a number within the range one to 29. He was not able to count backwards and as a consequence could not give the number which came before a number. He was shown numeral cards to identify and was proficient in identifying the numbers up to ten. However, he had difficulties with the larger numbers especially the teens. For example, he said 'twenty' for 12 and 'fifty' for 15. He also failed to identify decade numbers.

When assessed on the additive tasks 5 + 4 and 8 +3 he portrayed the same behaviours as Denise. He guessed. He was not able to solve tasks involving partially covered collections and he did not appear to be interested in trying to find a solution. He was successful, however, in demonstrating one-to-one correspondence with collections of 13 and then 18 units.

Collectively the three children have some proficiency in saying the forward number word sequence into the high twenties but all experience problems with teen and decade numbers. Judy and Denise can count backwards from ten but Michael is lost here. The lack of facility with number word sequences is also shown in the poor skills at saying the number which comes after or before a number word. Judy can identify numerals up to 20 but Denise and Michael's numeral identification skills are good only in the 1–10 range. Of the three children, Judy shows the most advanced strategy for the addition of two screened collections by the fact that she counts from one to arrive at the total. However, this is still a low-level strategy. Denise and Michael could not solve these problems, nor when they were posed using partially screened collections. However, they did have one-to-one correspondence. Overall it is clear that they are performing at a low level of numeracy given the standard that is expected for their year group.

Our experience in assessing children in the three countries has led us to believe that Judy, Denise and Michael are not unusual in their level of mathematical knowledge. We are sure that teachers everywhere will readily be able to substitute the name of one, or more, of their children for the above.

Nor is the problem being neglected. The desire to raise standards of numeracy is a stated national education priority for many nations. Certainly Australia, the USA and England are currently undertaking systemic initiatives in early mathematics and numeracy.

In Australia, for example, the Commonwealth Government is working jointly with the states and territories to establish agreed National Numeracy Benchmarks for 8-year-olds. Commonwealth, State and Territory ministers responsible for education have agreed the following literacy and numeracy goals: 'That every child leaving primary school should be numerate, and be able to read, write and spell at an appropriate level. That every child commencing school from 1998 will achieve a minimum acceptable literacy and numeracy standard within four years.' (*Numeracy = Everyone's Business, Numeracy Education Strategy Development Conference*, Adelaide, May 1997)

In the USA the Standards 2000 Project has released the National Council of Teachers of Mathematics updated Standards entitled *Principles and Standards for School Mathematics*. The publication includes ten standards for children's learning which span pre-school through to grade 12. The Standards emphasize how learning should grow across the four grade bands – K–2, 3–5, 6–8 and 9–12 – and are seen as statements of criteria for excellence in school mathematics. Standard 1: Number and Operation, for example, states

Mathematics instructional programmes should foster the development of number and operation sense so that all students –

- understand numbers, ways of representing numbers, relationships among numbers, and number systems
- understand the meaning of operations and how they relate to one another
- use computational tools and strategies fluently and estimate appropriately.

(Discussion Draft, October 1998)

In the UK the government has launched the National Numeracy Strategy which sets out a Framework for Teaching Mathematics (Department for Education and Employment, DfEE, 1999a). The Framework provides a year-on-year list of key objectives that are expected to be attained by the 'great majority' of children.

Examination of the published documents reveals a commonality in describing numerate children. The publications indicate the need for children to be confident and competent in working with numbers, money and measurement. Statements, listing the skills, knowledge and understanding to be attained, show that children should be able to calculate accurately and efficiently, both mentally and on paper, and have a sense of the size of a number and where it fits in the number system. They should have a knowledge of number facts and have strategies for solving problems. They should also be able to check the reasonableness of an answer and be able to explain their methods. The should recognize when it is appropriate to use calculators and have the skills to use them effectively.

We cannot disagree with these aims though clearly Judy, Denise and Michael are considerably behind in meeting the targets. While the aims are laudable it is, however, less clear how the improvement in attainment is to be achieved. How will the aims be translated into action to help Judy, Denise and Michael? The UK government's National Numeracy Strategy has embarked on a rigorous training programme and has published guidance on teaching mental calculation strategies (Qualifications and Curriculum Authority, QCA, 1999a), exemplification of key learning objectives (QCA, 1999b), sample lessons (NNP, 1999) and lists of associated mathematical vocabulary (DfEE, 1999b). Let us now examine this initiative in greater detail.

The UK National Numeracy Strategy

The National Numeracy Strategy's Framework for Teaching Mathematics (DfEE, 1999a) provides a year-on-year list of key objectives which are expected to be attained by the 'great majority' of children. The expectation is that the national strategy will raise the standards in numeracy so that by 2002, 75 per cent of children will reach the national average standard for Year 6. In 1998, the national average was 58 per cent and therefore an annual rate of growth of 4 per cent must be achieved. Each local education authority has been given a target for improvement. The LEAs in turn have set targets for individual schools.

The National Numeracy Strategy has also provided schools with a mechanism for attaining the objectives based upon best practice from European and Pacific-rim countries. The mechanism is a structured three-part daily mathematics lesson. The sections are referred to as Introduction, Main Teaching Activity and Plenary.

A typical lesson commences with five to ten minutes' oral work and mental calculation with the whole class, which is conducted at a brisk pace. The aim here is to rehearse, sharpen and develop mental and oral skills that may be called upon in the lesson. This is followed by the main teaching activity lasting 30–40 minutes where the teacher works directly on new input with the whole class. They then have the opportunity to split into group work or individual and paired work, thus providing consolidation and differentiation. The lesson concludes with a plenary session where the children explain their work, discuss the efficiency of different solution strategies and share misconceptions. It is also the opportunity for the teacher to help the children to assess their developing skills against the targets they have been set and to record their progress, to make links with other work and to set homework.

Even if the target is reached by 75 per cent of the children, by implication 25 per cent will fail. There is a danger, already apparent in the educational press, that schools will concentrate on the children who are likely to attain the desired level. Opposing views are also evident, giving warnings that struggling pupils will fall still further behind thus increasing the danger of social exclusion. Because the prominence in the strategy is being placed on whole-class introductions and summaries, with additional emphases on pace, mental agility and articulation of solutions and method, there is a concern that children such as Judy, Denise and Michael, who are less advanced and less confident, will not be able to participate fully. These children may continue to experience failure and begin to feel that they are not part of the classroom community.

The National Numeracy standards indicate that children at Year 1 should have the following understanding of numbers and the number system, calculations and problem-solving skills:

1. Count reliably at least 20 objects
2. Count-on and back in ones from any small number and in tens from and back to zero
3. Read, write and order numbers from 0 to at least 20; understand and use the vocabulary for comparing and ordering these numbers
4. Understand the operation of addition, and subtraction (as 'take away' and 'difference') and use the related vocabulary
5. Know by heart all pairs of numbers with a total of ten
6. Within the range 0 to 30, say the number that is one or ten more or less than any given number.

(QCA, 1999a, p. 6)

Clearly though Judy, Denise and Michael could meet no. 1, and partially meet nos. 2, 3 and 6, they could not meet no. 5 and only Judy has a strategy for addition and this is a low-level one. Our concern is that the approach described may well raise standards overall but it does not give sufficient detail, nor provide the less confident teacher with support firmly grounded in theory, to help the less able children at Year 1.

Help for Judy, Denise and Michael: the Mathematics Recovery Programme

The picture is not one of despondency, though. Judy, Denise and Michael and their respective Year 1 teachers did receive help, support and training. Each in their own country was selected to participate in the Mathematics Recovery Programme. A key feature of this programme is that it provides teachers with an extensive professional development course to improve their understanding, knowledge and skill in the teaching and assessment of early numeracy. This is achieved through participation in intensive, individualized teaching programmes for low-attaining Year 1 children. The skills learned on the one-to-one basis can then be applied to groups and whole classes of children.

Before explaining the short-term intervention programme in full detail let us exemplify how it helped our three children.

Judy Revisited

Following the assessment Judy received individual teaching sessions of 25 minutes' duration, four times per week, for a total of seven weeks. This was a total of 7 hours and 40 minutes. The teaching activities had the purpose of enhancing Judy's knowledge of the number word sequence and numerals, and to further develop her strategies for adding and subtracting. In selecting teaching activities the teacher's intention was to present problems that, on the one hand were quite challenging, but also were reasonably likely to be solved by the child. For the first three weeks of the teaching cycle Judy continued to adhere to her count-from-one strategy to solve addition and subtraction tasks.

During the fourth week of the teaching cycle Judy made a significant development in her strategies for adding and subtracting – she developed a strategy of counting-on rather than counting from one. Judy seemed to become aware of counting-on during her solution of the task of 20 + 3, which was presented verbally using two screened collections. She solved this task by counting from one to twenty and then continuing her counts from twenty-one to twenty-three, while keeping track of three counts. In an ensuing discussion with her teacher after having solving the task, Judy said 'twenty and three (pause), twenty-three!' Her statement seemed indicative of mental reflection on her solution to the task. From that point onward Judy routinely used counting-on to solve addition tasks and subtraction tasks. By the time of the fourth week of her teaching session Judy had also developed proficiency with the number word sequence in the range one to one hundred. Judy could now use counting-on to solve addition tasks presented verbally (that is, without use of written symbols), for example 87 + 5, and subtraction tasks presented verbally such as 42 + [ ] = 46.

By the end of the fourth week of the teaching cycle, it was apparent Judy had made significant progress in her early number knowledge, and there was little doubt that her progress was attributable to her participation in the MR teaching sessions. Also apparent was a very significant and positive change in Judy's general attitude to the MR teaching sessions. It was clear that Judy was keenly aware of her progress and success in Mathematics Recovery, and this awareness was accompanied by a very positive attitude towards participating in the teaching sessions. In her initial interview and in the early teaching sessions Judy tended to be somewhat quiet and withdrawn. Over the course of the teaching cycle there was a gradual and substantial change in her general disposition. By the time of the fourth week, for example, she seemed to relish undertaking tasks and solving problems. She would as much as challenge her teacher to present a difficult problem. Judy's MR teacher was fully aware of this change in Judy's attitude to the teaching sessions. Her classroom teacher observed that Judy was performing better in mathematics, exhibited an increased confidence in her approach to mathematics activities in the classroom and was more positive in her approach to all classroom activities.

Denise Revisited

Meanwhile Denise, in England, received four 25-minute lessons each week for a period of ten weeks. During that time she learned to count forwards and backwards from 112. She could say the number that came before, or after, a number in the range 1–100. She still had some hesitancy with certain decade numbers. She could identify all two-digit numerals and, like Judy, had developed a count-on strategy proudly exclaiming that she did not need to use her fingers. Denise's teacher had developed a game where a numeral card was turned over and a die was thrown to generate a subtraction problem. Denise turned over 14 and then threw a six.

Denise: That is a hard one, taking six away. I don't think I want to see that!
           (Denise counts up to six.)
Denise: Took 14 away, 13 away, 12 away, 11 away, 10 away, 9 away, 8.
           (As Denise was counting back she made a regular six pattern on the table.)

Denise had developed a count-down-from strategy which she used to explain how she answered 18 − 5 = [ ].

Three lessons later Denise's teacher hid 14 bears in a cave. She told Denise there were 14 bears and asked her to close her eyes as she was going to remove some bears. She did this and informed Denise that there were only 11 bears left in the cave. How many had gone out? This can be summarized as a missing subtrahend 14 – [ ] = 11 and is a very challenging task.

Denise: Three!
Teacher: How did you do that?
Denise: I jumped in my head. Because 14 is not a jump we go 13, then 12, then 11.

Denise later solved 16 to 13, 20 to 16, 27 to 25 and 30 to 26. For 16 to 13 she showed double counting skills as she counted down to.

Denise: 15 that's one, 14 that's two, 13 that's three.

Denise had advanced her numerical skill and strategies for addition. She was now adept at counting-on and could count up to for missing addends. She had a count-down-from strategy for subtraction and was beginning to develop a count-down-to strategy though as yet she did not always choose the most appropriate strategy to solve a particular problem. Like Judy, she grew in confidence and enthusiasm. Most pleasing to see was the way in which she relished the challenge of mathematics and her ability to articulate her strategies.

Michael Revisited

Michael received a similar teaching programme to those of Judy and Denise. He showed tremendous gains in arithmetical strategies, in forward and backward number word sequences, and in numeral identification, all of which impacted on his self-confidence. When he was being assessed at the end of the programme he said, 'I'm going to do good thinking this time.' He was presented with a very difficult symbolic subtraction problem. The task on the card was 16 – 12. He read the problem out loud without hesitation.

Teacher: Do you have a way of figuring that out?
            (Michael looked at the problem for about 15 seconds thinking hard. He looks up and says) Four.
Teacher: How did you figure that out?
            (Michael shrugs his head and smiles broadly.)
Teacher: Your mouth was moving.
Michael: I took away 12 and there was four.
            (As he was saying this he made a clenched fist with his left hand. His thumb and knuckles are facing him. He points to the little finger and says) Eleven was right there.

What is significant about this is that Michael was demonstrating a count-down-to strategy. He knew where 12 was and that if it had been 'subtract eleven' the answer would have been five. Michael also developed some 'known facts' which he used in addition and subtraction. Overall he showed considerable gains in strategies. His parents were delighted with the progress he had made and wished to share in it. Michael regularly took home a homework and communication book for numeracy. The lessons for the three children were routinely videotaped. Michael's parents watched some of the taught sessions to gain an understanding of the tasks and how they could reinforce the learning. Needless to say Michael does not receive special education remediation and he has exceeded the standard expected of his age group.

It can be said that any child receiving individualised teaching should make progress. However, the progress of all three children, in different contexts and educational systems, is highly significant. They have achieved considerable gains and now possess advanced strategies for the solution of challenging addition and subtraction tasks. Also the Mathematics Recovery programme can be seen to have had a very significant influence on the children's attitude to learning and self-esteem. They no longer see themselves as failing. Moreover, the programme has changed teachers' perceptions of what can be achieved and they have delighted in the ability to move children on from low-level to advanced strategies. During their professional development training in assessment and teaching they taught children individually. The knowledge and techniques they learned have been applied to teaching groups and classes. In this way all children benefit.

2

The Learning Framework in Number

Development of Mathematical Recovery included the development of a learning framework for assessment and teaching in early number. In 1996, this framework, referred to as the Learning Framework in Number (LFIN), was adapted as the foundational and guiding framework for the Count Me In Too project.

The Learning Framework in Number is organized into three strands and spans ten aspects of children's early numerical knowledge. All ten aspects of LFIN are considered to be important in children's early numerical learning. Table 2.1 provides an overview of LFIN. The Stages of Early Arithmetical Learning (SEAL) (Strand A) is the basic or primary, and most significant, aspect of LFIN. The next most important are Base-Ten Arithmetical Strategies (Strand A) and the three aspects of Strand B. Each of these five aspects is presented in a tabulated form as a model. These models set out stages or levels of student progression and facilitate profiling of a child's numerical knowledge. The ten aspects of LFIN should be regarded as closely interrelated early number topics.

The Purpose of LFIN

Learning Framework in Number provides essential guidance for assessment and teaching in early numeracy. Also, because LFIN is organized into a framework, it provides directionality for teaching and indicates likely progressions in children's learning. Teachers using LFIN are able to develop teaching strategies that allow children simultaneously to work and progress on more than one strand of the framework. They have a clear idea of the extent of their children's knowledge in terms of the ten aspects of the framework and can use the framework to predict the types of advancements their children are likely to make. Thus LFIN provides a comprehensive and integrated framework for early numerical learning. This approach is in clear contrast to one in which the focus of teaching is a specific range of

23

Table 2.1   The Learning Framework in Number

Part A	Part B	Part C
Early Arithmetical Strategies	Forward Number Word Sequences	Other Aspects of
Base-Ten Arithmetical Strategies	and Number Word After	Early Arithmetical
	Backward Number Word Sequences	Learning
	and Number Word Before	
	Numeral Identification	
Stages:	**Levels:**	
Early Arithmetical Strategies	**Forward Number Word**	Combining and
	Sequences (FNWS)	Partitioning
	and Number Word After	
		Spatial Patterns and
0 Emergent Counting	0 Emergent FNWS	Subitising
1 Perceptual Counting	1 Initial FNWS up to 'ten'	Temporal Sequences
2 Figurative Counting	2 Intermediate FNWS up to 'ten'	
3 Initial Number Sequence	3 Facile with FNWSs up to 'ten'	Finger Patterns
4 Intermediate Number	4 Facile with FNWSs up to 'thirty'	Base-Five (Quinary-
Sequence		Based) Strategies
5 Facile Number Sequence	5 Facile with FNWSs up to 'one	
	hundred'	
Levels:	**Levels:**	
Base-Ten Arithmetical	**Backward Number Word Sequences (BNWS)**	
Strategies	**and Number Word Before**	
1 Initial Concept of Ten	0 Emergent BNWS	
2 Intermediate Concept of Ten	1 Initial BNWS up to 'ten'	
3 Facile Concept of Ten	2 Intermediate BNWS up to 'ten'	
	3 Facile with BNWSs up to 'ten'	
	4 Facile with BNWSs up to 'thirty'	
	5 Facile with BNWSs up to 'one	
	hundred'	
	Levels:	
	Numeral Identification	
	0 Emergent Numeral Identification	
	1 Numerals to 'ten'	
	2 Numerals to 'twenty'	
	3 Numerals to 'one hundred'	
	2 Numerals to 'one thousand'	

numbers, for example first numbers 1–10, then 11–20 and, finally, 21–100.

The integrated nature of LFIN can be demonstrated as follows. A child solves an addition task, for example 7 + 4, by counting-on, a strategy that is classified in the Stages of Early Arithmetical Learning, an aspect of Strand A. In solving the task the child uses the forward number word sequence, that is 'seven, eight, nine, ten', which is an aspect of Strand B and uses their fingers to keep track of their counting. Use of finger patterns is an aspect which appears in Strand C.

Glossary

In order for the reader to become familiar with LFIN it is necessary to learn a range of technical terms. These terms relate mainly to children's early numerical knowledge and strategies, and associated instructional techniques. By and large these terms are explained in the following section. Additionally, for the convenience of the reader, explanations of these terms appear in the Glossary at the end of this book.

LFIN: Strand A

Aspect A1: Stages of Early Arithmetical Learning

As stated earlier, SEAL is considered the primary or most important aspect of LFIN. It is introduced in this chapter and explained and exemplified in Chapters 4 and 5. Finally, Chapter 7 includes applying SEAL in the analysis of children's assessment interviews.

Stages of Early Arithmetical Learning sets out a progression of the strategies children use in early numeracy situations that are problematic for them, for example being required to figure out how many in a collection, and various kinds of additive and subtractive situations. The SEAL model appears in Table 2.2 and consists of a progression of five stages in children's development of early arithmetical strategies. The label 'Stage 0' is used for children who have not attained the first stage. The SEAL model has been adapted from research by Steffe and colleagues (Steffe, 1992a; Steffe and Cobb, 1988; Steffe *et al.*, 1983) and related research by Wright (1989; 1991a). Finally, descriptions in the SEAL model include reference to particular tasks (e.g. Missing Addend) and strategies (e.g. count-on). Descriptions of these tasks and strategies are provided in the main Glossary at the end of this book, and more extensive explanations appear in Chapter 3.

Aspect A2: Base-Ten Arithmetical Strategies

Around the time they attain Stage 4 or 5 on the SEAL, children typically begin to develop knowledge of the tens and ones structure of the numeration system. Of course, children can and should solve addition and subtraction tasks involving two-digit numbers long before

Table 2.2   Model for Stages of Early Arithmetical Learning

Stage 0: Emergent Counting. Cannot count visible items. The child either does not know the number words or cannot co-ordinate the number words with items.

Stage 1: Perceptual Counting. Can count perceived items but not those in screened (that is concealed) collections. This may involve seeing, hearing or feeling items.

Stage 2: Figurative Counting. Can count the items in a screened collection but counting typically includes what adults might regard as redundant activity. For example, when presented with two screened collections, told how many in each collection, and asked how many counters in all, the child will count from 'one' instead of counting on.

Stage 3: Initial Number Sequence. Child uses counting-on rather than counting from 'one', to solve addition or Missing Addend tasks (e.g. $6 + x = 9$). The child may use a count-down-from strategy to solve Removed Items tasks (e.g. $17 - 3$ as 16, 15, 14 – answer 14) but not count-down-to strategies to solve Missing Subtrahend tasks (e.g. $17 - 14$ as 16, 15, 14 – answer 3).

Stage 4: Intermediate Number Sequence. The child counts-down-to to solve Miissing Subtrahend tasks (e.g. $17 - 14$ as 16, 15, 14 – answer 3). The child can choose the more efficient of count-down-from and count-down-to strategies.

Stage 5: Facile Number Sequence. The child uses a range of what are referred to as non-count-by-ones strategies. These strategies involve procedures other than counting by ones but may also involve some counting by ones. Thus in additive and subtractive situations, the child uses strategies such as compensation, using a known result, adding to ten, commutativity, subtraction as the inverse of addition, awareness of the 'ten' in a teen number.

they develop knowledge of the tens and ones structure. For children who have attained Stage 5, development of knowledge of the tens and ones structure becomes increasingly important. Table 2.3 outlines a progression of three levels in children's development of base-ten arithmetical strategies. The model for the development of base-ten arithmetical strategies is adapted from research by Cobb and Wheatley (1988).

LFIN: Strand B
The three aspects in Strand B are concerned with important specific aspects of children's early number knowledge: Forward Number Word Sequences (FNWSs), Backward Number Word Sequences (BNWSs), and Numeral Identification. These three aspects are described in this section and in Chapter 7 the models associated with these aspects are

Table 2.3 Model for the development of base-ten arithmetical strategies

Level 1: Initial Concept of Ten. The child does not see ten as a unit of any kind. The child focuses on the individual items that make up the ten. In addition or subtraction tasks involving tens, children count forward or backward by ones.

Level 2: Intermediate Concept of Ten. Ten is seen as a unit composed of ten ones. The child is dependent on re-presentations (like a mental replay or recollection) of units of ten such as hidden ten-strips or open hands of ten fingers. The child can perform addition and subtraction tasks involving tens where these are presented with materials such as covered strips of tens and ones. The child cannot solve addition and subtraction tasks involving tens and ones when presented as written number sentences.

Level 3: Facile Concept of Ten. The child can solve addition and subtraction tasks involving tens and ones without using materials or re-presentations of materials. The child can solve written number sentences involving tens and ones by adding or subtracting units of ten and ones.

Note: A necessary condition for attaining Level 1 is attainment of at least Stage 3 in the Stages of Early Arithmetical Learning.

applied in the analysis of children's assessment interviews. These models resulted from research by Wright (1991b; 1994). Finally, the assessment of these three aspects is discussed in Chapter 3.

Understanding children's specific strategies on tasks relating to these aspects is still important but perhaps less so than in the case Aspect A1, that is SEAL. There is also less emphasis on the idiosyncratic nature and diversity of the strategies relating to these aspects.

Aspects B1 and B2: FNWSs and BNWSs

The term 'number words' refers to the spoken and heard names of numbers. In LFIN an important distinction is made between counting and reciting a sequence of number words. This distinction was made by Steffe and Cobb (1988). The term 'counting' is used only in cases that involve co-ordination of each spoken number word with an actual or imagined (that is, conceptualized) item. Thus counting typically occurs in situations that are problematic for students, for example solving an additive or subtractive problem or establishing the numerosity of a collection of items. The activity of merely saying a sequence of number words is not referred to as counting.

The term 'Forward Number Word Sequence' refers to a regular sequence of number words forward, typically but not necessarily by ones, for example the FNWS from one to twenty, the FNWS from eighty-one to ninety-three, the FNWS by tens from twenty-four. The term 'Backward Number Word Sequence' is used in similar vein, for example the BNWS from twenty to ten. From the point of view of fully understanding children's early numerical knowledge, it is useful to construe as distinct the two aspects concerned with number word sequences, that is, forward and backward. Nevertheless, because of the many similarities between these two aspects their presentations here are integrated to some extent. Models associated with these aspects are shown in Tables 2.4 and 2.5. The label 'Level 0' is used for children who have not attained the first level.

Aspect B3: Numeral Identification

Numerals are the written and read symbols for numbers, for example '3', '27', '360'. Learning to identify, recognize and write numerals can rightly be regarded an important part of early literacy development. At the same time it is important to realize that this learning is equally,

Table 2.4 Model for the construction of Forward Number Word Sequences

---

Level 0: Emergent FNWS. The child cannot produce the FNWS from 'one' to 'ten'.

Level 1: Initial FNWS up to 'ten'. The child can produce the FNWS from 'one' to 'ten'. The child cannot produce the number word just after a given number word in the range 'one' to 'ten'. Dropping back to 'one' does not appear at this level. Children at Levels 1, 2 and 3 may be able to produce FNWSs beyond 'ten'.

Level 2: Intermediate FNWS up to 'ten'. The child can produce the FNWS from 'one' to 'ten'. The child can produce the number word just after a given number word but drops back to 'one' when doing so.

Level 3: Facile with FNWSs up to 'ten'. The child can produce the FNWS from 'one' to 'ten'. The child can produce the number word just after a given number word in the range 'one' to 'ten' without dropping back. The child has difficulty producing the number word just after a given number word, for numbers beyond ten.

Level 4: Facile with FNWSs up to 'thirty'. The child can produce the FNWS from 'one' to 'thirty'. The child can produce the number word just after a given number word in the range 'one' to 'thirty' without dropping back. Children at this level may be able to produce FNWSs beyond 'thirty'.

Level 5: Facile with FNWSs up to 'one hundred'. The child can produce FNWSs in the range 'one' to 'one hundred'. The child can produce the number word just after a given number word in the range 'one' to 'one hundred' without dropping back. Children at this level may be able to produce FNWSs beyond 'one hundred'.

Table 2.5 Model for the construction of Backward Number Word Sequences

Level 0: Emergent BNWS. The child cannot produce the BNWS from 'ten' to 'one'.

Level 1: Initial BNWS up to 'ten'. The child can produce the BNWS from 'ten' to 'one'. The child cannot produce the number word just before a given number word. Dropping back to 'one' does not appear at this level. Children at Levels 1, 2 and 3 may be able to produce BNWSs beyond 'ten'.

Level 2: Intermediate BNWS up to 'ten'. The child can produce the BNWS from 'ten' to 'one'. The child can produce the number word just before a given number word but drops back to 'one' when doing so.

Level 3: Facile with BNWSs up to 'ten'. The child can produce the BNWS from 'ten' to 'one'. The child can produce the number word just before a given number word in the range 'ten' to 'one' without dropping back. The child has difficulty producing the number word just before a given number word, for numbers beyond ten.

Level 4: Facile with BNWSs up to 'thirty'. The child can produce the BNWS from 'thirty' to 'one'. The child can produce the number word just before a given number word in the range 'one' to 'thirty' without dropping back. Children at this level may be able to produce BNWSs beyond 'thirty'.

Level 5: Facile with BNWSs up to 'one hundred'. The child can produce BNWSs in the range 'one hundred' to 'one'. The child can produce the number word just before a given number word in the range 'one' to 'one hundred' without dropping back. Children at this level may be able to produce BNWSs beyond 'one hundred'.

---

if not more so, an important part of early numerical development. The term 'identify' is used here with precise meaning, that is, to state the name of a displayed numeral. The complementary task of selecting a named numeral from a randomly arranged group of displayed numerals is referred to as 'recognizing'. Thus we make the distinction between 'numeral identification' and 'numeral recognition'. Using these terms in this way accords with typical use in psychology and in early literacy. Table 2.6 outlines a progression of four levels in children's development of numeral identification. As with the models above, the label 'Level 0' is used for children who have not attained the first level. (See also Chapter 3.)

LFIN: Strand C
By and large, the aspects in Strand C are not addressed specifically in the MR assessment. Nevertheless they often arise incidentally in children's solutions to tasks on the assessment. Thus these aspects should be regarded as interrelated with the aspects in Strands A and

Table 2.6   Model for the development of Numeral Identification

---

Level 0: Emergent Numeral Identification. Cannot identify some or all numerals in the range '1' to '10'.

Level 1: Numerals to '10'. Can identify numerals in the range '1' to '10'.

Level 2: Numerals to '20'. Can identify numerals in the range '1' to '20'.

Level 3: Numerals to '100'. Can identify one and two digit numerals.

Level 4: Numerals to '1000'. Can identify one, two and three digit numerals.

B. There are also close interrelationships among the aspects within Strand C, for example combining and partitioning are interrelated with spatial patterns and finger patterns, temporal patterns are interrelated with spatial patterns and finger patterns are interrelated with the base-five aspect.

Each of the five aspects in Strand C is potentially important in children's early numerical development and descriptions of each follow. Because these aspects are not explicitly revisited in the later chapters focusing on assessment and its analysis, more extensive descriptions are provided here than were provided above for the aspects in Strands A and B. The description of each of the five aspects in Strand C typically includes examples of instructional tasks and children's strategies.

Aspect C1: Combining and Partitioning

Counting strategies are an important aspect of children's early numerical knowledge. Nevertheless, at the same time as they develop counting strategies, children may also develop knowledge of simple combinations and partitions of numbers, which does not rely on counting. Examples of these combinations are the addition of two numbers in the range one to five. Doubles of the numbers in the range one to five and beyond (e.g. four and four is eight) are prominent examples of these combinations. The process of partitioning (e.g. eight is four and four, six is four and two) is the complement of combining. Children learn to provide answers almost immediately to questions such as three plus three, using procedures that do not involve counting-by-ones. Numerical knowledge of this kind has been labelled 'automatized' or 'habituated'. Recent research provides strong indications that teaching children to habituate simple addition facts through combining and partitioning of small numbers can significantly facilitate development of advanced numerical strategies, that is non-count-by-one strategies. Combining and partitioning can also be important for the development of base-five strategies (see C5 below). Development of this aspect has drawn on research by Cobb and colleagues (Cobb, Wood and Yackel, 1991; 1992; Yackel, Cobb and Wood, 1991).

Instructional Tasks for Combining and Partitioning. The activities below involve either finger patterns and thus interrelate with Aspect C4 or spatial patterns and thus interrelate with Aspect C2. There is a wide range in the facility of young children to make finger patterns and to use fingers in solving numerical tasks. For some it will be necessary to raise their fingers slowly and sequentially in order to build a finger pattern for a number, and for some it will be necessary to observe their fingers when doing this. Others can raise their fingers simultaneously to build a finger pattern and will not need to observe their fingers. An excellent instructional technique is to direct children to place their hands on their heads when undertaking the activities (this activity is referred to as 'Rabbits' ears'). In this way children are not able to observe their own fingers when making the patterns although some children may need to move their hands into their field of vision.

1. *Doubling using finger patterns.* Ask the child to show three and three, that is three on each hand. How many in all?
2. *Combining numbers using finger patterns.* Ask the child to raise stated numbers of fingers on each hand, for example four and two, and to say how many in all.
3. *Partitioning with fingers.* Ask the child to show a total of four, for example, on two hands. Ask the child to do the task in several ways.
4. *Flashing spatial patterns.* Briefly display a pattern consisting of, for example, three red and three blue. Ask how many red, how many blue, how many in all?
5. *Partitioning spatial patterns.* Briefly display a pattern for seven, all of one colour. Ask the child to partition the pattern into two numbers. Ask the child to partition in several ways.

Linking to Base-Five Knowledge (Aspect C5). The tasks above can be modified to focus specifically on base-five strategies (see Aspect C5 below). The following list gives examples of these modifications for tasks involving finger patterns:

- Use two hands to show combinations that make five.
- Partition five using two hands.

- Use two hands to make combinations of the form $5 + n$, for numbers in the range six to ten, for example $5 + 4$.
- Partition numbers in the range six to ten into $5 + n$, for example eight is shown as five fingers on one hand and three on the other.

Aspect C2: Spatial Patterns and Subitizing

This aspect relates to strategies that arise in situations involving spatial configurations of various kinds, for example domino patterns, pairs patterns, Tens Frame, playing card patterns, regular plane figures and random arrays. Activities involving spatial patterns and subitizing have an important role in young children's numerical development.

Subitizing: Background and Definitions

Subitizing is a technical term in psychology. The *Penguin Dictionary of Psychology* defines 'subitize' thus: 'To apprehend directly the number of dots in an unstructured stimulus display without counting them. The limit on this process is about seven or eight dots.' Von Glasersfeld (1982) described subitizing as 'the immediate, correct assignation of number words to small collections of perceptual items'. In his discussion of subitizing von Glasersfeld points out that when a young child says, for example, 'three' in response to a briefly displayed spatial array, the child may be doing no more than recognizing and naming a spatial arrangement. One cannot assume that this child has a concept of 'three'. Nevertheless being able to name spatial arrays in this way is an important basis. No doubt at some point the child will see a correspondence between the name of the array, that is 'three', and the last number word when they count the dots in the array, for example 'one, two, three'.

Subitizing and Spatial Patterns. 'Subitizing' is a technical term with a specific meaning whereas, in the context of early arithmetic, the term 'spatial patterns' is more general or more inclusive. In early number there is a range of instructional settings for which spatial pattern or spatial arrangement seems to be a dominant feature. These include dot cards with random or irregular arrays, the various dots cards with regular patterns (see below); rows of counters arranged by twos or fives and with colour differentiating each group of ten, the Tens Frame, plane figures (triangles, squares, etc.).

Dot Cards with Regular Patterns. These include domino patterns for

1 to 6, pairs patterns for 1 to 10, and others such as a 3 × 3 array of dots for nine, and a triangle of dots for 3. The last mentioned is not exactly the same as the pairs pattern for 3, and the domino patterns for two and three are arranged diagonally rather than vertically or horizontally. Each number from one to ten could also be represented with a 'five pattern'. This would refer to the patterns that arise when numbers are represented using the top row of the Arithmetic Rack (see Glossary at the end of this book), for example four is OOOO and eight is OOOOOXXX (that is using two colours). Finally, the patterns on the playing cards (from one to 13 on the extended pack) constitute another interesting example. In the range one to six they correspond with the domino patterns more or less, although the patterns for two and three are vertical rather than diagonal.

Aspect C3: Temporal Sequences

Temporal sequences involve events that occur sequentially in time, for example sequences of sounds and movements. Sequences of sounds may be rhythmical, arrhythmic or monotonic. Instructional settings in which the child's task is to count or copy a sequence of sounds or count a sequence of movements are considered likely to enhance early numerical knowledge. There has been little systematic study of children's strategies associated with temporal sequences. Experience has shown that, as a general rule, children are not as facile at counting temporal sequences as they are at counting items occurring in spatial sequence, for example rows of counters or dots. For example, in contrast to counting a row of counters, when counting a sequence of sounds the child has no control of the speed of perception of the individual items. Development of this aspect has drawn on research by Wright (e.g. 1989).

Children's Strategies. Children will count slow monotonic sequences of sounds and sequences of movements similarly to the way they count a row of items, that is, to co-ordinate a number word in sequence with their perception of each item. When counting rapid, rhythmical sequences of up to six sounds any one of three strategies might be used:

1. counting the individual sounds from one as they occur;
2. recognizing the pattern in terms of its number of beats and thus answer without counting; and
3. mentally replaying or re-presenting the pattern, after its completion, and counting the number of beats in re-presentation.

Aspect C4: Finger Patterns

Using one's fingers is very prominent in early number. Fingers are used in a range of ways and with varying levels of facility and sophistication. An example of a reasonably advanced strategy is using fingers to keep track of counting-on. Thus in working out 7 + 4, a child might raise four fingers sequentially in co-ordination with saying 'eight, nine, ten, eleven'. The fingers serve the purpose of keeping track of the count and the child stops at eleven because they realize that they have made four counts and this is indicated by having four fingers raised. An example of a less advanced strategy is when a child works out 4 + 3 by sequentially raising four fingers on one hand in co-ordination with counting from one to four, then raises three fingers on the other hand in co-ordination with counting from one to three and, finally, counts their raised fingers from one to seven. In the latter case the child does not have a facile finger pattern for three or four and necessarily establishes finger patterns for these numbers prior to working out 4 + 3. As children progress across the SEAL they typically develop increasingly sophisticated finger strategies. One expects ultimately that children will no longer rely on using finger patterns. Nevertheless finger patterns play an important role in early numerical strategies, and their use and development is to be encouraged.

Instructional Tasks and Strategies Involving Finger Patterns

Explicitly Requested Finger Patterns. The child is asked to use their fingers to show a number in the range one to ten or to use their fingers to show two numbers in the range one to five and to work out how many all together.

1. *Making numbers on the fingers.* The teacher asks the child to show various numbers on their fingers. This is best done in random rather than numerical order, first in the range one to five and then six to ten: 'Show me four on your fingers', similarly, two, five, one, three, then seven, nine, six, ten and eight. Of interest is whether the child raises the fingers sequentially while counting from 'one' or raises their fingers simultaneously, for example raising four fingers simultaneously to show 'four'. Also of interest is the extent to which it is necessary for the child to observe their fingers.

2. *Showing numbers where fingers cannot be seen.* The child is instructed to put their hands above their head. This task involves making a number in the range from one to five on each hand and figuring out how many altogether, e.g. one and one, two and

two ... five and five, two and one, etc. A total of 25 combinations can be asked in this way. As before these should be presented in random order. Of particular interest here is the child's strategy for working out the sum. Does the child count from 'one' or count on from one of the addends? If counting on, how does the child keep track of the second addend. Does this involve moving a finger in co-ordination with each uttered number word, for example? The task four and three, for example, might involve lowering each finger on the hand showing three, in sequence with saying the words 'five, six, seven'. The child may need to place their hands in front of them to see their fingers in order to work out the answer. In this case the child is likely to count from 'one'. An alternative is to count-on from the number of fingers shown on one hand. A variation of this task is for the teacher to first make and display a pattern, that is the teacher places their hands above their head, the teacher then removes the displayed pattern, and then asks the child to copy it and work out the sum.

Spontaneous Use of Fingers on an Additive Task. The following three examples show a progression from less to more sophisticated use of finger patterns for addition. Progressing from the first to the second or the second to the third involves curtailment (see Glossary at the end of this book) of the strategy.

1. *Counting forward from one three times using fingers for addition.* On a task such as four and two the child says the number words from 'one' to 'four' in sequence with raising four fingers. This is followed by saying the number words from 'one' to 'two' in sequence with raising two fingers. Finally, the child counts their raised fingers from 'one' to 'six'. The last count is likely to involve some means of keeping track of the fingers counted, for example lowering each of the six raised fingers in turn, touching each finger in turn on the face or desk or using each hand in turn to 'tick off' the fingers of the other hand.
2. *Simultaneously raising fingers for the first addend and then the second.* In the case of an additive task, children will simultaneously raise fingers on one hand to signify the first stated addend and then simultaneously raise fingers on the other to signify the second.
3. *Using fingers to keep track of counting-on when solving an additive task.* In the case of 12 + 4, the child raises four fingers

sequentially in sequence with uttering the number words 'thirteen' to 'sixteen'. The fingers serve to keep a record of the number of forward counts from 'thirteen'. Implicit in this method is that the child can recognize their finger pattern for 'four' and by this means, determine when the count is complete.

Spontaneous Use of Fingers on Subtractive Tasks. In similar vein the following three examples show a progression from less to more sophisticated use of finger patterns for subtractive tasks.

1. *Counting forward from one three times using fingers for subtraction.* On a task such as eight take away five the child says the number words from 'one' to 'eight' in sequence with raising eight fingers. This is followed by saying the number words from 'one' to 'five' in sequence with lowering five fingers. Finally, the child says the number words from 'one' to 'three' while lowering the three raised fingers in turn.
2. *Simultaneously raising fingers for the minuend and then lowering fingers for the subtrahend.* In the case of a subtractive task, children will simultaneously raise fingers to signify the minuend. This is followed by lowering fingers for the subtrahend. This may be simultaneous or sequential, for example for the subtrahend of seven, five fingers are simultaneously lowered and then two more are sequentially lowered.
3. *Using fingers to keep track of counting when solving subtractive tasks.* Children will use fingers to keep track of counting-up-to on a Missing Addend task; counting-down-from on a Removed Items task; and counting-down-to on a Missing Subtrahend task. (These tasks and strategies are described in Chapter 3.)

Aspect C5: Base-Five (Quinary-Based) Strategies

These strategies involve using the number five as a base and arise in instructional settings involving the arrangement of items in fives, for example the Arithmetic Rack and the Tens Frame, and also settings where use of fingers is prominent (that is because there are five fingers on each hand). Using five as a base means that combining and partitioning of numbers involving five is given special emphasis in children's learning, and is therefore likely to be incorporated by children into additive and subtractive strategies. Typically in these settings, the number ten is also a base, for example two rows of five can be seen as ten. Thus five does not replace ten as a base. Rather, five is an additional base. In early number there is a major potential advantage associated with five being used as an additional base along with ten, that is using five as a base has the potential to greatly reduce reliance on counting-by-ones. Development of this aspect has drawn on research by Gravemeijer (1994).

Examples of base-five strategies are: working out 3 + 4 by saying 'three and two is five, and two more is seven' and working out 8 – 4 by saying 'eight take three is five and one more back is four'. Development of base-five strategies is closely linked to the development of combining and partitioning strategies (see Aspect C1 above). In the first example just discussed (3 + 4), 4 is partitioned into 2 and 2, and in the second example (8 – 4), 4 is partitioned into 3 and 1. Promoting the use of base-five strategies in early number is considered likely to facilitate development of advanced numerical strategies and to support children's advancement across the stages of SEAL.

Examples of Base-Five Strategies.

1. *Going through 'five' strategy for addition.* To work out three plus six the child says three and two make five, and four more make nine.
2. *Partitioning 'five' strategy.* To work out five minus two the child partitions five into three and two, and thus answers three without needing to count by ones.
3. *Partitioning numbers greater than 'five' strategy.* To work out eight minus three the child partitions eight into five and three and thus answers five without needing to count by ones.
4. *Going through 'five' strategy for subtraction.* To work out seven minus four the child partitions seven into five and two, and then says four and one more make five, and five and two more make seven.

Extending Base-Five Strategies. The strategies described above can be extended by children in various ways to involve base-ten. For example, to solve eight plus four, eight and two is ten and two more is twelve, and to solve twelve minus five, twelve minus two is ten, and ten minus three is seven.

Summary

The Mathematics Recovery Programme was developed in Australia in order to address the problem of chronic failure in school mathematics and to address the need for early intervention in number learning.

Mathematics Recovery was developed via a nationally funded research programme and since 1995 has been extended to the USA and the UK, and has been successfully applied to classroom mathematics on a large scale, for example via the Count Me In Too project, and also individually by schools participating in MR. The programme involves individualized teaching, on a daily basis, of low-attaining first-grade students. Mathematics Recovery teaching is problem based and routinely involves children in periods of intensive and sustained thinking about number problems and reflecting on the results of their thinking.

The Learning Framework in Number provides a basis for assessment and teaching in MR and related programs such as Count Me In Too. LFIN consists of ten interrelated aspects of early number, which are organized into three strands: Strand A – the Stages of Early Arithmetical Learning and tens and ones knowledge; Strand B – forward and backward number word sequences and numerals; and Strand C – combining and partitioning, spatial patterns, temporal sequences, finger patterns, and base-five strategies. Strand A (SEAL) is the most important aspect in LFIN and relates to the relative sophistication of the child's strategies for counting, adding or subtracting. The five aspects in Strands A and B are set out in tabular form (Table 2.1) showing a progression of stages or levels. Determining the child's stages and levels results in a comprehensive profile of the child's early number knowledge.

3

Mathematics Recovery Assessment

In this chapter we introduce the distinctive approach to assessment used in MR. The assessment is administered individually and focuses on identifying the child's most sophisticated numerical strategies, as well as facility with number words and numerals. The interrelationships between the assessment and LFIN are explained in detail. The chapter concludes with detailed descriptions of exemplary tasks for assessment and teaching and descriptions of strategies used by children to solve these tasks. Specific instructions required to prepare for and administer the assessment interview are in Chapter 6, and the directions for coding and analysing the assessment interview are in Chapter 7.

Observation and Assessment

Underlying the development of MR and the Learning Framework in Number is a belief that in early number learning it is very important to understand, observe and take account of children's knowledge and strategies. Children's early numerical knowledge varies greatly and their strategies are multifarious. Thus, across children, early numerical knowledge is characterized by both commonalities and diversity. As indicated by the research of Denvir and Brown (1986a, 1986b), it is insufficient to think that every child's early numerical knowledge develops along a common developmental path. For example, one important factor in a particular child's developmental path, it is believed, relates to the nature of the settings in which the child's prior learning has occurred. Also, children who may appear to an observer to be in the same setting or learning situation will construct the situation idiosyncratically and thus different kinds of learning are likely to occur.

The child's process of constructing numerical knowledge can be thought of in terms of progression or advancement. Children reconstruct or modify their current strategies and doing so is nothing more or less than progression, advancement or learning. Given this, it is useful to consider the notion of the relative sophistication of children's strategies. For example, the child who has no means of working out nine plus three other than counting out nine counters from one, counting out three counters from one, and then counting all of the counters from one to 12, is using a less sophisticated strategy than the child who ignores the counters and says nine plus three is the same as ten plus two, and I know that is 12 without counting.

Settings, Tasks, Strategies and Procedures

The term 'task' is used as the generic label for particular problems or questions presented to a child in an assessment or teaching session, while 'setting' is used as the generic label for physical situations used by the teacher in posing a task. Examples of tasks are: given two screened collections of counters, asking the child how many counters in all; asking the child to say the number words from 'twenty' to 'ten'; asking the child to hold up four fingers on each hand and say how many in all. Examples of settings are: a row of numeral cards, two piles of counters, a Tens Frame, a Hundreds Chart, etc. A 'strategy' is a particular method by which a child solves a task. A 'procedure' is a part of a strategy, and strategies consist of one or more procedures. Thus a child's strategy for solving the task of 8 + 4 may involve the procedure of counting from 'one' to 'eight', and the procedure of counting from 'nine' to 'twelve' in co-ordination with sequentially raising four fingers to keep track. Also, specific procedures may be part of differing strategies, and specific procedures may be relevant to more than one of the aspects of early number. For example, the procedure of raising fingers in turn to keep track of counting-on is relevant to the aspects of numerical strategies (A1) and finger patterns (C4).

Presenting Tasks

A necessary part of determining a child's strategies is to present the child with tasks or situations which are problematic for her or him. In such situations the child's goal, we assume, is to resolve the difficulty, that is, to solve the problem as he or she constructs it. In doing so the child uses a current strategy or may construct a strategy that is novel for that child. It is not essential that the tasks presented to children be what adults might label as 'real-world' or everyday situations. For example, it can be just as useful and productive to pose a problem about numbers, number words or numerals *per se*, as to pose a problem about an everyday situation. Observations of children's solutions to a range of numerical problems leads to an understanding of the range, diversity and progression of children's strategies. With such knowledge teachers are able to determine a profile of numerical knowledge for each child.

Eliciting Strategies

It is important to note that children frequently use strategies that are less sophisticated than those of which they are capable. This may happen for one or more of several reasons, for example:

1. it may be easier and although it may take more time, this may not be of concern to the child; or
2. some feature of the child's thinking immediately prior to solving the current task may focus the child's attention on a less sophisticated strategy.

Thus an important challenge for the teacher as observer and diagnostician is to attempt to elicit the child's most sophisticated strategy. This is crucial to fully understand the extent of the child's current knowledge. Eliciting a strategy is not necessarily the same as asking the child to describe their strategy, after he or she has solved a problem. Close observation and informed reflection while interviewing are crucial to understanding a child's strategy. Asking a child to describe a strategy is sometimes useful but, equally, can be off-putting for the child, particularly if this becomes a routine directive. When asked to describe a strategy just used, a child may also unwittingly or intentionally describe a strategy different from the one used.

Overview of MR Assessment

Mathematics Recovery involves a distinctive approach to assessing young children's numerical knowledge. The origins of this method are in research projects conducted in the 1980s amd 1990s that focused on understanding children's numerical strategies and the modifications children make to their strategies over time (e.g. Cobb and Steffe, 1982; Steffe and Cobb, 1988; Steffe *et al.*, 1983; Wright, 1989; 1991a). Since 1992, this approach to assessment has been used successfully by hundreds of teachers in the UK, the USA and Australia.

The assessment in MR is interview based and involves presenting the child with numerical tasks and observing the child's responses. The assessment interview is videotaped and the teacher does not attempt to record the child's responses during the course of the interview. Rather, the teacher observes the child's responses and strategies closely and poses and modifies follow-up tasks on the basis of their observations. The teacher may also ask the child to explain the strategy that they have used. Analysis of the child's performance on the assessment involves replaying the videotaped interview and coding the child's responses using an assessment schedule. Experience has shown that the process of videotaping assessment interviews constitutes a rich source of professional learning for teachers.

Mathematics Recovery assessment consists of two separate schedules of tasks, Assessment A (Table 3.1) and Assessment B (Table 3.2). Assessment A is used first and Assessment B is administered at a later session to children who, on the basis of their performance on Assessment A, are assessed at Stage 3 or higher on SEAL. The tasks in Assessment A were developed in research projects by Steffe *et al.* (1983) and Steffe and Cobb (1988) and Wright (1989; 1994; 1996). The tasks used in Assessment B were developed in research projects by Cobb *et al.* (Cobb and Wheatley, 1988; Cobb, Wood and Yackel, 1991; 1992).

Mathematics Recovery: Assessment A

Assessment A consists of nine Task Groups (i.e. groups of tasks). One important outcome of the assessment is the determination of the child's Stage of Early Arithmetical Learning and the child's levels on the other models in Strands A and B of LFIN (see Chapter 2). Table 3.3 sets out the Task Groups from Assessment A and indicates for which of the models each Task Group is relevant. As can be seen in Table 3.3, Task Group 3 (Subitizing) and Task Group 7 (Sequencing Numerals) do not correspond to any of the models. These are included because they can provide additional information about the child's numerical knowledge and strategies.

Overview of Tasks in Assessment A

As stated above, one important outcome of the assessment is the determination of the child's stage and levels. The assessment also provides extensive information about the child's numerical knowledge, including their strategies, strengths, difficulties, etc. This kind of information is particularly useful in informing future teaching and helps teachers to gain a greater appreciation of the richness of children's numerical knowledge. Thus it is important to keep in mind that the purposes of the assessment are broader than merely determining the stages and levels. Task Groups 1 to 7 on Assessment A are mainly concerned with assessing the child's facility with number word sequences and numerals and mainly relate to the models of FNWS, BNWS and Numeral Identification. Task Groups 8 and 9 are concerned with assessing the child's early numerical strategies and relate to the SEAL model. The task groups are described below in more detail and terms such as 'Introductory Examples' and 'Entry Tasks' are also explained.

Table 3.3 Task Groups and associated models for Assessment A

Task Groups		Model
1.	Forward Number Word Sequence	FNWS
2.	Number Word After	FNWS
3.	Subitizing	
4.	Numeral Identification	Numeral Identification
5.	Backward Number Word Sequence	BNWS
6.	Number Word Before	BNWS
7.	Sequencing Numerals	
8.	Additive Tasks	SEAL
9.	Subtractive Tasks	SEAL

Task Groups 1 and 2

In the FNWS tasks (Task Group 1) the child's task is to say the number word sequences starting from one or a given number word, as directed by the teacher. This is a familiar activity for many children. In the Number Word After task the child states the number word after a given number word within a particular range, for example 1 to 10. As indicated in Table 3.3, the tasks in Groups 1 and 2 provide assessment information that enables the interviewer to determine the child's level of FNWS development. The tasks in Task Groups 1 and 2 are discussed in more detail later in this chapter (see 'Assessing Aspects of Strand B').

Task Groups 5 and 6

The tasks in Task Groups 5 and 6 are similar to the tasks in Task Groups 1 and 2 respectively. Thus in Task Group 5 the child is asked to say BNWSs and in Task Group 6 the child states the number word before a given number word within a particular range. Task Groups 5 and 6 provide assessment information for determining the level of BNWS development. The BNWS tasks (Task Groups 5 and 6) are not presented immediately after FNWS tasks (Task Groups 5 and 6). This serves to reduce the possibility of the child confusing forward and backward number word tasks, that is, confusing number word after with number word before or confusing FNWSs with BNWSs. The tasks in Task Groups 5 and 6 are discussed in more detail later in this chapter (see 'Assessing Aspects of Strand B').

Task Group 4
Task Group 4 involves the child identifying a numeral which the teacher displays. Task Group 4 also enables the interviewer to determine the child's level of Numeral Identification. Numeral Identification tasks are discussed in more detail later in this chapter (see 'Assessing Aspects of Strand B').

Task Groups 3 and 7
The Subitizing tasks (Task Group 3) relate to Aspect C2 in LFIN. Of interest in these tasks is whether the child can identify (i.e. ascribe number to) regular and irregular spatial patterns, the range of numbers for which patterns can be identified and, in the case of incorrect answers, how close the child's answer is to the correct answer. Task Group 7 assesses the child's ability to correctly order sequences of numeral cards. Children's solutions of the tasks in Task Group 7 are likely to draw on their FNWS knowledge as well as their numeral identification knowledge, and thus these tasks can provide interesting additional insights into these aspects of children's numerical knowledge. Tasks Groups 3 and 7 are not directly concerned with determining the child's stage or levels.

Task Group 8
Task Group 8 focuses on the child's strategies when solving counting, additive tasks and Missing Addend tasks, and contributes to determining the child's stage (i.e. in terms of SEAL). The additive tasks in Task Group 8 involve two collections of counters with one or both of the collections being screened. The Missing Addend tasks also involve the use of screened collections. These tasks are discussed in more detail later in this chapter (see the section on exemplary instructional tasks for counting and early addition and subtraction). Also discussed in more detail are the strategies that children use to solve these tasks (see the section on advanced count-by-ones strategies).

Task Group 9
Task Group 9 focuses on the child's strategies when solving three different kinds of subtractive tasks and also contributes to determining

the child's stage (i.e. in terms of SEAL). The first task involves pre-senting '16 – 12' in a written form. This task is relatively advanced and is likely to be the most difficult of the subtractive tasks. The task is presented in order to provide a situation where the child may exhibit an advanced strategy, for example a part or parts of the strat-egy may involve other than counting-by-ones. The task is presented before the other subtractive tasks because, during the course of an interview, children are likely to continue using strategies that are suc-cessful. Thus if the task of '16 – 12' is placed later in the interview a child who has used counting-by-ones to solve an earlier subtractive task successfully, might use counting-by-ones out of habit almost, rather than a more advanced strategy, to solve '16 – 12'. The main purpose of the Missing Subtrahend tasks is to elicit the strategy of 'counting-down-to' and the main purpose of the Removed Items tasks is to elicit the strategy of 'counting-down-from'. As with all of the assessment tasks it is important for the interviewer to maintain an open frame of mind about the types of strategies the children use to solve these subtractive tasks. These tasks are discussed in more detail later in this chapter (see the section on exemplary instructional tasks for counting and early addition and subtraction). Also discussed in more detail are the strategies that children use to solve these tasks (see the section on advanced count-by-ones strategies).

Introductory Examples, Entry Tasks, etc.
On Assessment A an introductory example is included in some Task Groups. These have the purpose of providing a relatively simple example that serves to introduce the child to a new type of task. Some Task Groups are formatted into three sections headed Entry Task, Less Advanced Task and more Advanced Task. The child is first pre-sented with the items in the Entry Task section. If the child is gener-ally successful on these then the child is presented with the items in the More Advanced section. The items in the Less Advanced section are used in cases where the child is not successful on all of the items in the Entry Task section. In some cases it may be appropriate to present the tasks in all three sections, for example the child might answer quickly on the items in the Entry Task section but might make one or two errors. Finally, on Task Groups 8 and 9, Supplementary Tasks are provided and are used in cases where the interviewer is unsure of the kind of strategy the child has used on the entry tasks in that Task Group.

Mathematics Recovery: Assessment B

As stated earlier, Assessment B is administered at a later session to children who are assessed at Stage 3 or higher on the Stages of Early Arithmetical Learning. Assessment B's purpose is to provide information about the child's base-ten strategies and additional information about the child's early numerical strategies. Assessment B consists of three groups of tasks. Table 3.4 sets out the groups of tasks from Assessment B and indicates for which of the models each group of tasks is relevant.

Table 3.4   Task Groups and associated models for Assessment B

Group of Tasks	Model
10. Tasks to elicit non-count-by-one strategies	SEAL
11. Tens and ones tasks – strips	Base-Ten
12. Tens and ones tasks – uncovering	Base-Ten
13. Horizontal sentences	Base-Ten

Overview of Tasks in Assessment B

Assessment B is administered at a later session and only if the child has attained at least Stage 3 in terms of SEAL. Assessment B is concerned with Stage 5 on SEAL and the child's knowledge of tens and ones, that is Aspect A2 of LFIN.

Task Group 10

Task Group 10 is concerned with assessing the child's ability to use strategies which are characteristic of Stage 5 on SEAL. In the first four tasks (a–d) the child is first asked to solve a written task involving addition or subtraction. Following this the child is asked if they are able to use their solution to solve related tasks. Of interest is the extent to which the child uses a given number sentence to solve a related number sentence. In Task (a), for example, using the known result of '9 + 3 = 12' to solve '9 + 4', etc. is an example of a Stage 5 strategy. As stated above in the Overview of Tasks in Assessment A, the interviewer should keep an open frame of mind with regard to the kinds of strategies children might use on these tasks. The child might use an expected strategy to solve some of these tasks and use unexpected and idiosyncratic strategies to solve others. In determining whether the child is at Stage 5 the interviewer should take account of the child's use of Stage 5 strategies in these tasks and in the additive and subtractive tasks in Assessment A (i.e. Task Groups 8 and 9).

The child is judged to be at Stage 5 if, in Assessment A and B together, they provide a total of at least three instances of a Stage 5 strategy. This is explained in detail in Chapter 7.

Task Groups 11–13

Task Groups 11–13 are concerned with Aspect A2 of LFIN, that is, Base-Ten Arithmetical Strategies. Thus these tasks indicate to what extent the child might use strategies that incorporate knowledge of the tens and ones structure of two-digit numbers and the types of strategies the child might use. These tasks enable the determination of the child's level in terms of the model for the Development of Base-Ten Arithmetical Strategies.

Task Group 11

Task Group 11 involves the use of Ten Strips. A Ten Strip is a strip of cardboard containing a row of ten dots. The purpose of these tasks is to determine whether the child can increment by tens in situations where the Ten Strips are displayed rather than screened and each increment is by one ten only. The interviewer places the strips on the table one at a time, and the child's task is to say how many dots there are after each new strip is placed on the table. On the first task the number of dots is 10, 20, 30, etc. The second task commences with a Four Strip (i.e. a strip containing four dots only), and thus the number of dots is 4, 14, 24, etc.

Task Group 12

Task Group 12 involves the use of large sheets containing rows of ten dots and rows containing fewer than ten dots. The sheets are progressively uncovered and the child's task relates to describing the number of uncovered dots in all. These are referred to as the uncovering tasks and involve increasingly complex ways of incrementing by tens and/or ones.

Task Group 13

The first task in Task Group 13 is presented in similar vein to the tasks in Task Group 10. In the remaining tasks in Task Group 13 the child's task is to solve problems involving two-digit addition or subtraction presented in written format.

Determining the child's level

In Task Groups 11–13, children are judged to be at Level 1 if they are unable to increment by tens in the tasks involving base-ten materials, that is, Task Groups 11 and 12. Children are judged to be at Level 2 if they are able to increment by tens in the tasks involving base-ten materials but are unable to do so in the tasks that do not involve base-ten materials, that is Task Group 13 involving written number problems. To be judged at Level 2 the child would be expected to increment by tens on both tasks in Task Group 11, and to increment appropriately in both tasks in Task Group 12, but it is not necessary for the child to correctly answer each task. Finally, children are judged to be at Level 3 if they are able to increment by tens when solving the tasks that do not involve base-ten materials, that is, the horizontal sentences. It is not necessary for children to correctly answer each of these tasks.

Exemplary Instructional Tasks for Counting and Early Addition and Subtraction: Linking Tasks and Strategies

The first part of this section provides detailed examples of instructional tasks that are relevant to counting and early addition and subtraction. Some of the types of tasks which appear below are also included in Mathematics Recovery Assessment A. The purpose of this section is to provide a comprehensive and detailed listing of basic instructional tasks. All the tasks listed below can be used in formal and informal assessment, and can be adapted in various ways for individualized or class instruction.

The particular strategies that children use to solve these tasks can be dependent on the size of the numbers used in the tasks. For this reason, where relevant, the descriptions of the additive and subtractive tasks include specification of the sizes of the numbers to be used in the tasks. There are important links between particular additive and subtractive tasks and the strategies that children are likely to use to solve those tasks. In other words, the task is considered likely to elicit a particular strategy. These strategies are indicative of Stage 3 or Stage 4 and are referred to collectively as 'advanced count-by-ones strategies'. This is described in the second part of this section. The third part of this section lists examples of 'non-count-by-ones strategies', that is, Stage 5 strategies.

Instructional Tasks Related to the Stages of Early Arithmetical Learning: Tasks Involving Visible Items in a Collection

1. *Counting items in a collection.* This is a basic and very common assessment task in early number work. The child is given a

collection of counters, for example 8, 15 or 27, and asked to count how many in all. Of interest are whether the child knows the number words themselves and whether the child correctly co-ordinates the number words with the items.

2. *Producing a collection of specified number.* Like the first task listed above, this task is widely used in early number assessment and is in a sense complementary to the first task. The child is presented with a collection of, say, 50 counters, and is asked to count out a specified number of counters, for example 5, 10, 23, etc.

Tasks Involving Visible Items in a Row

1. *Counting items in a row.* This is a useful variation on the previous task, and can be presented by placing out a row of counters or using long strips of cardboard containing rows of circular stickers.

2. *Counting items in a row forward and backward.* In this task the child is asked to count forward and backward using a row as described in the previous task. This task assesses the child's facility with saying the number words forward or backward in co-ordination with items.

Additive Tasks Involving Two Collections of Screened Items

1. *Counting items of two collections one of which is screened.* This task involves two collections one of which is screened. For example, six counters are placed in front of the child, displayed briefly and then screened. Three counters are then placed to the right of the six screened counters. The child is asked how many counters there are altogether. Initially the numbers of counters in each collection should conform to the following: the first collection is in the range four to ten, and the second collection is in the range one to four.

2: *Counting items of two collections both of which are screened.* This task involves two screened collections. For example, six counters are placed in front of the child, displayed briefly and then screened. Three counters are similarly placed to the right of the six screened counters, displayed and then screened. As before, the child is asked how many counters there are altogether. Initially the numbers are similar to that described for the previous task. The number in the first collection can be extended to any two-digit number and the number in the second collection should usually be no larger than six. This facilitates the use of the counting-up-from (also known as counting-on) strategy (see the discussion of advanced count-by-ones strategies later in this section).

Subtractive Tasks

The types of subtractive tasks used in MR teaching are Missing Addend, Removed Items, Missing Subtrahend and Comparison. The first three of these are important in the MR assessment. Each of these tasks is described in detail below and a method of coding each kind of task is provided. The codes constitute a concise way to refer to specific tasks. As indicated earlier, the sizes of the numbers in these tasks are likely to influence the strategies used by children to solve the tasks.

Missing Addend Task

Task Code: 6 to 9

In this example, 6 is the known addend, 3 is the missing addend and 9 is the known sum.

Use 6 red and 3 green counters. Briefly display and then screen the known larger addend, that is 6 red counters. 'Here are six red counters.' Place out and screen, without displaying, the unknown smaller addend, that is 3 green counters. 'Here are some green counters and with those red counters there are nine altogether. How many green counters are there?'

The known addend is larger than the unknown addend and initially is typically in the range 6 to 12. The smaller addend is typically in the range 1 to 4. The known larger addend can be extended to any two-digit number depending on the child's facility with FNWSs. The unknown smaller addend is typically in the range 1 to 6. This facilitates the use of the counting-up-to (also known as counting-on) strategy (see the discussion of advanced count-by-ones strategies later in this section).

Removed Items Task

Task Code: 9 remove 3 (or 9 r 3)

In this example 9 is the known minuend, 3 is the known subtrahend and 6 is the unknown difference. Use 9 counters of one colour. Briefly display and then screen the 9 counters. 'Here are nine counters.' Remove, briefly display and then screen 3 counters, thus leaving 6 counters screened. 'I had nine counters to begin with and then I took three away. How many counters are left there?'

The known subtrahend is smaller than the unknown difference.

Initially the known minuend is typically in the range 6 to 12. The known subtrahend is typically in the range 1 to 4. The known minuend can be extended to any two-digit number depending on the child's facility with FNWSs and BNWSs. The known subtrahend is typically in the range 1 to 4. This facilitates the use of the counting-down-from strategy (see the discussion of advanced count-by-ones strategies later in this section).

Missing Subtrahend Task
Task Code: 9 to 6

In this example 9 is the known minuend, 6 is the known difference and 3 is the unknown subtrahend. Use 9 counters of one colour. Briefly display and then screen the 9 counters. 'Here are nine counters.' Remove and screen 3 counters leaving 6 counters under the other screen. 'I had nine counters to begin with and then I took some away and now there are six. How many counters did I take away?'

The unknown subtrahend is smaller than the known difference. Initially the known minuend is typically in the range 6 to 12. The unknown subtrahend is typically in the range 1 to 4. The known minuend can be extended to any two-digit number depending on the child's facility with FNWSs and BNWSs. The unknown smaller addend is typically in the range 1 to 4. This facilitates the use of the counting-down-to strategy (see the discussion of advanced count-by-ones strategies later in this section).

Comparison Task
Task Code: 9 compared with 6 (or 9 c 6)

In this example, 9 is the known minuend and 6 is the known subtrahend. This task differs from the previous three because it involves a comparison of two collections rather than partitioning one collection into two parts.

Use 9 red counters and 6 green counters. Briefly display and then screen the 9 red counters. 'Here are nine red counters.' Briefly display and then screen the 6 green counters. 'Here are six green counters. How many more red counters are there than green counters?'

The unknown difference is smaller than the known subtrahend. Initially the known minuend is typically in the range 6 to 12. The unknown difference is typically in the range 1 to 4. The known minuend can be extended to any two-digit number depending on the child's facility with FNWSs and BNWSs. The unknown smaller addend is typically in the range 1 to 4. In MR sessions, comparison tasks were observed to elicit a wider range of strategies than the other subtraction tasks. Thus no specific strategy is associated with this task.

Comparison Task: Alternative Presentation
Use 9 counters and 6 small cubes (e.g. side of length 1 cm). Briefly display and then screen the 9 counters. 'Here are nine horses.' Briefly display and then screen the 6 cubes. 'Here are six jockeys. If I put a jockey on each horse how many horses would not have a jockey?'

Advanced Count-By-Ones Strategies (Stages 3 and 4)
This section provides descriptions of the prominent strategies used by children on some of the additive and subtractive tasks that appear in the previous section. By and large, each strategy can be regarded as being elicited by a particular task. The counting-down-to strategy, which is characteristic of Stage 4, is conceptually more advanced than the other three, which are characteristic of Stage 3. Of course, children who use counting-down-to are likely to use the other strategies because, as has already been explained, the strategies are task dependent. On the other hand, one should expect to find children who use one or more of the first three strategies but do not use counting-down-to.

Counting-Up-From (Stage 3)
This strategy is typical on additive tasks involving two screened collections, for example 6 and 3. The child says: 'Six, . . . seven, eight, nine . . . Nine!' The essential feature is that the child counts on from 'six'. The child knows in advance the number of counts. Inherent in this strategy is keeping track of three counts. This may involve explicit double counting, for example seven is one, eight is two, etc., or may involve sequentially raising three fingers in co-ordination with saying the number words from 'seven' to 'nine'. Alternatively the child has and uses a concept of three number words in temporal sequence. In this case saying 'seven, eight, nine' is recognized as three counts. The child anticipates that she can make three counts after 'six'.

Counting-Up-To (Stage 3)
This strategy is typical on Missing Addend Tasks: Task Code: 6 to 9.
The child says: 'Six . . . seven, eight, nine . . . three!' The essential feature is that the child counts on from 'six'. As before, this strategy involves keeping track of counts but the child does not know in advance the number of counts. Rather, the child knows in advance where she is counting to. This may involve explicit double counting

similar to but differing from that in the previous case. The difference may not be apparent to the observer. As before, the child may sequentially raise three fingers or may use a concept of three number words in temporal sequence.

Counting-Down-From (Stage 3).

This strategy is typical on the Removed Items tasks: Task Code: 9 remove 3.

The child says: 'Nine . . . eight, seven, six . . . six!' This strategy involves keeping track of backward rather than forward counts and the child knows in advance the number of counts.

Counting-Down-To (Stage 4).

This strategy is typical on Missing Subtrahend tasks: Task Code: 9 to 6.

The child says: 'Nine . . . eight, seven, six . . . three!' This strategy involves keeping track of backward counts. In this case the child does not know in advance the number of counts. Rather, she knows in advance where she is counting to.

Non-Count-By-One Strategies (Stage 5)

The strategies described below are characteristic of children who have attained Stage 5 on the model for the Stages of Early Arithmetical Learning. The child at Stage 5 and also the child at Stage 4 are likely to be comfortable with additive and subtractive tasks presented in written format, rather than using collections of counters.

- *Compensation for addition.* Six plus four is the same as five plus five.
- *Compensation for subtraction.* Nine take away four is five because eight take away four is four.
- *Commuting for addition.* Two and nine is the same as nine and two.
- *Using addition for subtraction.* Four and four are eight so eight take away four is four.
- *Using doubles.* Five and five is ten so five and four is nine.
- *Using a known fact.* Seven and three are ten so seven and four are eleven.
- *Addition by partitioning using five as a base.* Four and three is the same as four and one and two.
- *Subtraction by partitioning using five as a base.* Seven take away four is seven take two – five, and five take two – three.

- *Addition using ten as a base.* Seven and six is the same as seven and three – ten, and three more – thirteen.
- *Subtraction using ten as a base.* Fifteen take away four is eleven because fifteen take away five is ten and four is one less than five.

Assessing Aspects of Strand B

This section has the purpose of describing in greater detail the tasks used in the assessment of the three aspects of Strand B. The section includes explanation of the assessment of children's facility with FNWSs and number word after tasks; with BNWSs and number word before tasks; and with numeral identification and numeral recognition.

FNWS Tasks

The purpose of these tasks is to assess the child's facility with the forward number word sequence. To begin the teacher says: 'start counting from "one" please'. When the child reaches 'thirty-two' the teacher directs the child to stop. This is followed by similarly assessing parts of the number word sequence beyond the 'thirties'. For example, the teacher says, 'start counting from "forty-eight" please'. The teacher directs the child to stop on reaching 'sixty-one'. A particular purpose with this task is to assess if the child can continue beyond 'forty-nine'. Similarly, 'start counting from "seventy-six" please' (stop at 'eighty-four'). In the case of a task such as 'start counting from ninety-two' of particular interest are: (a) what the child says after 'ninety-nine', and if the child continues, what they say after 'one hundred and ten', etc.

Number Word After Tasks

These tasks assess the child's ability to say the number word after a given number word. On a task such as 'what comes after seven?', we want to observe whether the child: (1) says 'eight' immediately or soon after being asked; (2) says the number word sequence forward from 'one' aloud or subvocally – referred to as a dropping-back strategy; or (3) is unable to answer. We begin these tasks by asking the word after several number words in the range 'one' to 'ten'. These are presented in a random order within the following ranges: 'one' to 'ten'; 'eleven' to 'thirty'; 'thirty' to 'one hundred'. Of particular interest are words for numbers with '9' or '0' in the ones place, for example 'twenty-nine', 'fifty', 'sixty-nine'.

BNWS Tasks

In this case we begin by asking the child to count from 'ten' back to 'one'. This is followed by 'fifteen' back to 'ten' and 'twenty' back to 'ten' and 'thirty' back to 'twenty'. For many children, all but the first of these will be difficult or impossible. Some children are able to do these but do so slowly and with what appears to be a good deal of mental effort. The interviewer needs to observe carefully for signs of fatigue or distress in the child. As in the case of the forward number word sequence, backward sequences in the range 'thirty' to 'one hundred' are also assessed.

Number Word Before Tasks

These tasks assess the child's ability to say the number word before a given number word. On a task such as 'what comes before nine?', we want to observe whether the child: (1) says 'eight' immediately or soon after being asked; (2) says the number word sequence forward from 'one' aloud or subvocally – referred to as a dropping-back strategy; or (3) is unable to answer. We begin these tasks by asking the word before several number words in the range 'one' to 'ten', presented in a random order, and then similarly in the ranges 'eleven' to 'thirty'; and 'thirty' to 'one hundred'. Of particular interest are words for numbers with '0' or '1' in the ones place, for example 'sixty', 'thirty-one'.

Numeral Identification

Numeral Identification is assessed by displaying numeral cards individually and asking the child to say the name of the numeral. Guidelines for presenting these tasks are:

1. The numerals are not displayed in numerical sequence.
2. Numerals in a specific range are assessed in turn, that is numerals in the range '1' to '10', '11' to '20', '21' to '100', '101' to '1000'.
3. In the ranges '1' to '10' and '11' to '20', most or all of the numerals may be tested.
4. Children who can identify the numerals in the range '11' to '20' can almost certainly also identify numerals in the range '1' to '10'. Thus one may begin by assessing numerals in the range '11' to '20' and if the child succeeds at these it is not necessary to assess numerals in the range '1' to '10'.
5. It is not practical to test all the numerals in the ranges '21' to

'100' and '101' to '1000'. In these ranges a sample of numerals should be tested. The sample should include but not be limited to particular or special cases, for example decade numerals (e.g. '40', '70' and '100') and double-digit numerals (e.g. '66', '33' and '100'), three-digit numerals with '0' in the ones or tens place (e.g. '260', '703') or '1' in the tens place (e.g. 412).

Numeral Recognition

As indicated earlier, Numeral Recognition refers to the ability to select from a collection of numeral cards displayed in random order, the numeral card corresponding to a spoken number word. Numeral Recognition can be assessed in similar vein to Numeral Identification and the guidelines above apply equally to the assessment of Numeral Recognition.

Table 3.1   Assessment Interview A

Assessment Interview A

Name ....   DoB...

Class .... Teacher..............................   Age .... (years) .... (months)

Interviewer ....   Date of Interview .... /.............. /..............

	Arithmetical Strategies	FNWS	Numerical Identification	BNWS
Stage/Level				

1)   Forward Number Word Sequence

"Start counting from ** and I'll tell you when to stop."

a) 1 (to 32)	b) 48 (to 61)
c) 76 (to 84)	d) 93 (to 112)

2)   Number Word After

"Say the word that comes straight after **" Example: "Say the word that comes straight after 1".

a) entry task
14   11   19   12
23   29   20

b) less advanced task
5   9   7
3   6

c) more advanced task
59   65   32
70   99

3)   Subitizing and Spatial Patterns

Show each card briefly, for about half a second, saying, " I'm going to show you some cards very quickly. Tell me how many spots are on each one."

Regular	4	3	2	5	6
Irregular	3	6	2	7	4	5	8

4)   Numeral Identification

Show each card in turn, saying, " What number is this ?"

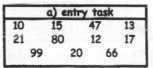

a) entry task
10   15   47   13
21   80   12   17
99   20   66

b) less advanced task
8   3   5
7   9   6
2   4   1

c) more advanced task
100   123   206
341   820

5)   Backwards Number Word Sequence

Example :   "Count backwards from 3." "3...2...1".   "Count backwards from ten to one"
                    "Now count backwards from ** and keep going until I say stop"

a) 10 (down to 1)	b) 15 (down to 10)	c) 23 (down to 16)
d) 34 (down to 27)	e) 72 (down to 67)	f) 100 (down to 91)

6) Number Word Before

"Say the word that comes just before **". Example : "Say the number that comes just before 2"

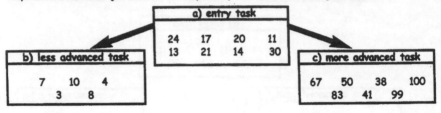

a) entry task

| 24 | 17 | 20 | 11 |
| 13 | 21 | 14 | 30 |

b) less advanced task

| 7 | 10 | 4 |
| | 3 | 8 |

c) more advanced task

| 67 | 50 | 38 | 100 |
| | 83 | 41 | 99 |

7) Sequencing Numerals

Show the ten numeral cards face up in random order, asking the child to identify each number as you put it out. Then say "Can you place the cards in order? Start by putting the smallest down here."

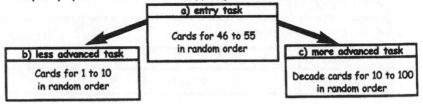

a) entry task

Cards for 46 to 55 in random order

b) less advanced task

Cards for 1 to 10 in random order

c) more advanced task

Decade cards for 10 to 100 in random order

8) Additive Tasks (Screened, use counters of two colours)

Example; "There are three counters under here, and two counters under here. How many counters are there altogether?"

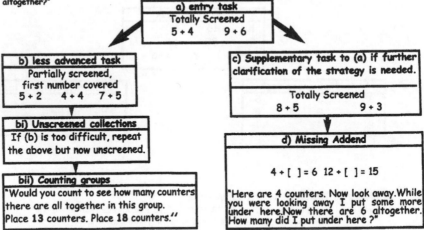

a) entry task
Totally Screened
5 + 4   9 + 6

b) less advanced task
Partially screened, first number covered
5 + 2   4 + 4   7 + 5

bi) Unscreened collections
If (b) is too difficult, repeat the above but now unscreened.

bii) Counting groups
"Would you count to see how many counters there are all together in this group.
Place 13 counters. Place 18 counters."

c) Supplementary task to (a) if further clarification of the strategy is needed.

Totally Screened
8 + 5   9 + 3

d) Missing Addend

4 + [ ] = 6   12 + [ ] = 15

"Here are 4 counters. Now look away. While you were looking away I put some more under here. Now there are 6 altogether. How many did I put under here ?"

9. Subtractive tasks

9.1 Present the task as a written number sentence on card. Say to the child " What does this say ? Do you have a way to work out what the answer is ?"

Entry Task	Supplementary Task
16 - 12	14 - 10

9.2 Missing Subtrahend

"Here are five counters." (Ask the child to look away. Remove and screen 2 counters). "There were five counters, but while you were looking away I took some and hid them under here (indicating screen) and now there are 3. (display briefly and screen). How many counters did I hide under here ?" (indicating screen).

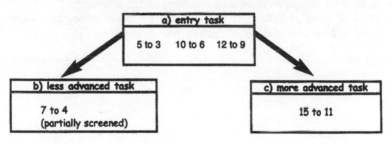

a) entry task

5 to 3   10 to 6   12 to 9

b) less advanced task

7 to 4
(partially screened)

c) more advanced task

15 to 11

9.3 Removed Items

"Here are three counters (briefly display, then screen). If I take away, (remove one counter, display briefly, then screen) how many are left under here ? "(indicate the first screen) i.e. 3 - 1 = ?

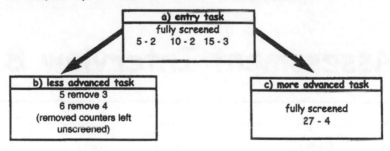

a) entry task
fully screened
5 - 2   10 - 2   15 - 3

b) less advanced task
5 remove 3
6 remove 4
(removed counters left
unscreened)

c) more advanced task

fully screened
27 - 4

Summary Guidelines for Presenting Assessment Tasks
1. Present the tasks in order which they appear in the schedule.
2. Avoid re-posing the task unless you are sure it is necessary.
3. Verbal instructions may be rephrased if it is likely to help the child understand the task.
4. Tasks may be revisited in situations where the child is thought to have made a random error.
5. Give the child sufficient time to focus on solving the task.
6. Avoid temptations to talk to the child when they are engaged in solving a task.
7. Watch closely for the finger, head and body movements that may provide insights into the child's thinking.
8. As a general rule do not comment on the correctness of the child's response.
9. Be sensitive to the child's state of ease and comfort during the course of the interview and use motivation and encouragement sparingly.
10. Use the technique of 'talking to the camera' if it likely to be particularly useful to record an observation or realisation.

Table 3.2 Assessment Interview B

Assessment Interview B

Name .... DoB..

Class .... Teacher................................. Age .... (years) .... (months)

Interviewer .... Date of Interview .... /............... /...............

	Stages of Early Arithmetical Learning	Tens and Ones
Stage		

10. Tasks to Elicit Non-Count-By-One Strategies

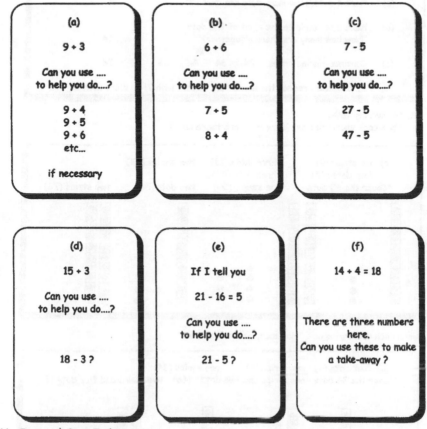

(a)	(b)	(c)
9 + 3	6 + 6	7 - 5
Can you use .... to help you do....?	Can you use .... to help you do....?	Can you use .... to help you do....?
9 + 4 9 + 5 9 + 6 etc... if necessary	7 + 5 8 + 4	27 - 5 47 - 5

(d)	(e)	(f)
15 + 3	If I tell you	14 + 4 = 18
Can you use .... to help you do....?	21 - 16 = 5	
	Can you use .... to help you do....?	There are three numbers here. Can you use these to make a take-away ?
18 - 3 ?	21 - 5 ?	

11. Tens and Ones Tasks

11.1 Counting by tens with 'Strips' - informal familiarisation of material

(a) "How many do we have ?" Put down strip. If the child says 'one', ask, "How many dots?"

(b) "How many altogether ?" Put down one strip at a time to 8 strips - 80 dots
   10   20   30   40   50   60   70   80

(c) Pick up all of the strips. "How many dots do we have?" "How many strips are there ?"

11.2 Incrementing by Ten

(a)	Place 4 dots."How many dots are there ?"	4
(b)	Place a ten strip to the right of the dots. "Now how many are there altogether?"	14
(c)	Continue placing strips. 24 34 44 54 64 74	
(d)	If necessary repeat the whole task - start with 7; or start with 3	

12. Uncovering tasks
Upon each uncovering ask "How many are there now ?"

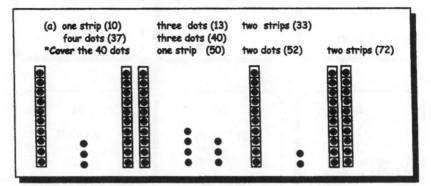

(a) one strip (10)   three dots (13)   two strips (33)
    four dots (37)   three dots (40)
*Cover the 40 dots   one strip (50)   two dots (52)   two strips (72)

Upon each uncovering ask, "How many are there now ?"

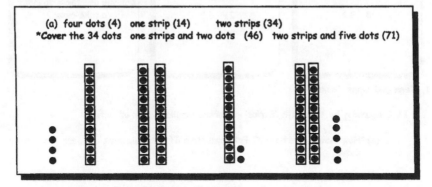

(a) four dots (4)   one strip (14)   two strips (34)
*Cover the 34 dots   one strips and two dots (46)   two strips and five dots (71)

13. Horizontal Sentences
"Do you have a way to figure out what this is ?"

(a) 16 + 10 = so what is ....? 16 + 9	(b) 42 + 23 =	(c) 38 + 24 =
(d) 39 + 53 =	(e) 56 - 23	(f) 43 - 15 =

4

The Stages of Early Arithmetical Learning

This chapter focuses on explaining and exemplifying the Stages of Early Arithmetical Learning. Progression across the stages involves the child using counting in increasingly sophisticated ways to solve additive and subtractive tasks. For each stage, two examples of children's solution attempts are presented. Each example consists of an objective description of the child's solution of one or several problems, and a discussion of the strategies used by the child in terms of SEAL.

The model of the Stages of Early Arithmetical Learning was introduced in Chapter 2. The model constitutes the primary and most important aspect of the Learning Framework in Number, and provides a model of increasingly advanced numerical strategies used by children in situations that involve counting, adding or subtracting. In this chapter, the origin and background of SEAL are explained. This explanation includes an introduction to the particular sense in which the term 'counting' is used in SEAL, explanations of the terms 'stages' and 'levels', and a discussion of the means by which children's numerical strategies may be observed. This is followed by a detailed description of each of the stages. Included in the description of each stage are two examples of children's problem-solving activity relevant to the stage. These examples take the form of video excerpts, that is, objective descriptions of the child's problem-solving activity. Each video excerpt is followed by a discussion of the problem-solving activity portrayed in the excerpt.

Overview of SEAL

The model of the Stages of Early Arithmetical Learning is based on a coherent body of research into young children's number learning undertaken by Steffe (Steffe, 1992; Steffe and Cobb, 1988; Steffe et al., 1983) and related research by Wright (1989; 1991a). This research involved longitudinal studies in which children were taught several times per week during teaching cycles of up to 20 weeks' duration, in their first and/or second years of school. An important focus of this research was the ways in which children's numerical strategies arose during enquiry-based teaching, and how these strategies developed and changed over the course of one or two years of school.

Teachers who have learned about and applied SEAL have found that it provides crucial directionality to their teaching. By applying SEAL in the observation and assessment of children these teachers have a sound knowledge of the child's current level in terms of the development of early arithmetical strategies. Also, SEAL provides a crucial framework for determining teaching activities that are optimal in the sense of leading to advancement in terms of SEAL, that is, advancements in which children reorganize their numerical thinking and construct novel strategies that, in a mathematical sense, are more sophisticated than their previous strategies.

Counting

Steffe *et al.* (1983) make a crucial distinction between counting and the mere utterance of number words in sequence – commonly referred to as 'rote counting'. Counting in the terms of Steffe *et al.* arises in problem-solving contexts, for example additive or subtractive situations. In these situations it is assumed that the child has a goal, for example figuring out how many counters there are in two screened collections, or how may counters remain under the screen when some have been removed. In the terms of Steffe *et al.* (1983) counting involves the co-ordination of each uttered number word with the conceptual production of a 'unit item'. The nature of this unit item changes according to the child's stage, that is in terms of SEAL. Steffe's notion of 'unit item' is particularly useful for observing and understanding the counting behaviour of children who are in Stage 2. This is discussed later in this chapter.

Stages and Levels

In the work of Steffe *et al.* (1983) the term 'stage' is used in a formal and theoretical sense to encompass four characteristics:

1. A characteristic remains constant for a period of time.
2. The stages form an invariant sequence.
3. Each stage builds on and incorporates the previous stage.
4. Each new stage involves a significant conceptual reorganization.

A level is regarded as a point in time rather than a period of time. The child has attained a level when he or she satisfies specific performance criteria for that level. This distinction between stage and level is explained in detail by von Glasersfeld and Kelley (1982). In the Learning Framework in Number, the term 'level' is used in the models which focus on the development of number word sequences, numeral identification, and knowledge of tens and ones, and the term 'stage' is used in the SEAL model, which is the focus of this chapter.

Observing Children's Strategies
Fundamental to the research on which SEAL is based is the notion that, in order to understand children's mathematical learning, it is crucial to closely observe their behaviour in problem-solving situations. In studying children's early numerical learning in particular, this observation focuses on children's verbal and non-verbal responses in situations in which they solve problems involving counting, addition or subtraction. These problems typically involve presenting children with a range of tasks involving counters that may be displayed or screened. These types of situations, that is, involving what adults might regard as trivial number problems, have been found to be extremely useful for the purpose of studying children's early numerical learning.

Explaining the Stages

In the remainder of this chapter, each of the Stages of Early Arithmetical Learning (SEAL) is explained. Included for each Stage are two illustrations of child problem-solving behaviour – each in the form of an objective description of an excerpt from a videotape of an assessment or teaching session. Each excerpt is followed by a discussion. In writing the discussion the author takes account of the videotape excerpt *per se*, rather than the description. Ten of the excerpts are based on Mathematics Recovery assessment sessions and two on MR teaching sessions. For purposes of clarification, this is stated at the beginning of the excerpt in the case of the two teaching sessions.

Stage 0: Emergent Counting
The work of Steffe *et al.* (1983) and Steffe and Cobb (1988) resulted in a five-stage model of the development of early arithmetical strategies, that is, strategies for counting, adding and subtracting. The first of these stages is given the label of 'perceptual'. In research projects conducted by Wright (1991b; 1994) prior to MR, it became apparent that among children in the first two years of school, there are a significant number who are not able to count a visible collection, for

example a collection of say 12, 15 or 18 counters. In MR the label 'emergent' was adopted for such children. The label 'Stage 0' is used to indicate children at this emergent level.

Video Excerpt 0.1: Heather and Larry

H: (Places out five red counters and screens them. Then places out four blue counters and screens them.) Five red counters and four blue counters. Can you tell me how many I have altogether this time?

L: (Immediately) Six.

H: Are you thinking? Five and four more. (Points to the screens in turn.)

L: (Thinks for a few seconds, looking up.) Umm.

H: How are you going to work out how many that makes?

L: (Sequentially raises the five fingers of his left hand. Then looks at his right hand while raising one finger.) How many is that?

H: Five on this one and four on this one. (Points to the screens in turn as before.)

L: (Sequentially raises four fingers on his right hand and then looks at his left hand.) One, two, three, four (wagging a finger in co-ordination with each count. Now looks at his right hand). Five. (Pauses.) Five, six, seven, eight! (Again wagging fingers in turn.)

H: (Removes both screens.) Have a look.

L: (Looks at the collection of five counters.) One, two, three, four. (In co-ordination with four points over the collection of five counters. Now looks at the collection of four counters. Points at one counter.) Five. (Pauses.) Five, eight, seven, eight! (In co-ordination with four points over the collection of four counters.)

H: (Places out 13 counters.) Can you tell me how many counters there are there altogether?

L: One, two, three . . . twelve. (Moves each of the 13 counters in turn but makes an error in co-ordinating his counts with his points.)

Discussion of Video Excerpt 0.1

Significant in the above excerpt is that, on three occasions, Larry does not correctly count visible items. When the screened collections of five and four are unscreened Larry counts 'eight' rather than 'nine'. When counting the collection of 13 counters, Larry counts 'twelve'. Additionally, Larry counts eight when counting his raised fingers, that is five on one hand and four on the other. On each of the three occasions

Larry is unable to properly co-ordinate his counts with the perceptual items, that is counters. Counting behaviour of this kind is illustrative of the child at the Emergent Stage.

Video Excerpt 0.2: Terry and Rita

T: What's three plus two? (Points to three unscreened counters and then to two unscreened counters.) How many would that be?

R: (Looks at Terry.) Equals.

T: What does it equal?

R: (Immediately.) Equals nine.

T: Nine do you think? (Points to both collections.) Do you think there are nine counters there?

R: Uhh, yeh!

T: I'm going to give you a group of counters Rita. (Places out 13 counters.) Can you tell me how many counters there are?

R: One, two, three . . . eleven. (Co-ordinates a number word with each count but omits to point at two of the counters.)

Discussion of Video Excerpt 0.2

In the above protocol Rita is presented with the task of 3 counters plus 2 counters with both collections unscreened. It is interesting to observe that Rita does not use a counting strategy to figure out how many counters altogether. She answers 'equals nine' but does not count. She does not spontaneously count the counters in this particular situation at least, that is with two separate collections – even though they are very small collections – 3 and 2. She does not seem to have this strategy available, that is, she does not seem able to conceive of the counters as forming or being reformed into one collection, for the purposes of establishing how many altogether. At this point Terry places out 13 counters and asks Rita to tell her how many counters there are. Rita counts from 'one' but does not correctly co-ordinate the number words with the counters. For this reason Rita is classified as Stage 0: Emergent Counting.

Children who are classified at Stage 0 are those who are not able to count perceptual items, that is they cannot co-ordinate number words with items when they count. When attempting to count 13 counters Larry points 13 times while saying the words from one to twelve. Larry's error is one of not co-ordinating his number words with his points. By way of contrast Rita correctly co-ordinates her number words with her points but omits two of the counters. A child may also be classified as Stage 0 if they cannot say the forward number word sequence, for example the child cannot count 13 counters because they do not know the number word sequence from one to thirteen. Rita's difficulty on the first task, that is, not having a strategy to establish the numerosity of two collections, for example not counting the collections, has been observed among children classified as being at Stage 0 (and also some children at Stage 1). Their lack of counting to solve these tasks is possibly attributable to an inability to conceptualize that two collections can alternatively be regarded as one collection.

Stage 1: Perceptual Counting

Children at Stage 1: Perceptual Counting are able to solve additive tasks involving material (e.g. counters) which is perceptually available (e.g. visible), that is tasks involving one collection or two collections of counters that are displayed rather than screened (Steffe *et al.*, 1983, pp. 22–3). Children at Stage 1 are unable to solve additive or subtractive tasks involving screened items. Children at Stage 1 are said to count 'perceptual unit items'.

In the video excerpt below, Amy solves tasks in which the counters are displayed but is generally unsuccessful on tasks in which counters are screened.

Video Excerpt 1.1: Mary and Amy

M: (Places out five blue counters and screens them.) Five counters there. (Places out two red counters leaving them unscreened.) And two counters there. How many altogether?

A: (Quickly.) Five! Eight.

M: (Removes the screen covering the five blue counters.) Want to check?

A: (Looks steadily at the desk on which counters are placed for five seconds and then looks up.) One.

M: (Waves hand over the counters.) How many altogether?

A: (Immediately.) Three.

M: Would you like to count them up?

A: (Points at one blue counter.) One. (Pauses and then moves the collection of two red counters adjacent to the collection of five blue counters.) One, two . . . seven. (Counts quickly while pointing to each counter in turn.)

M: This time, there are four counters there. (Places out four red counters and screens them.) And four counters there. (Places out a second collection of four red counters and leaves them unscreened.) How many altogether?

A: (Looks at the unscreened collection for five seconds.) One.
M: (Places her hand on the screen.) How many are under here?
A: (Immediately.) Four.
M: (Waves her hand over the unscreened collection.) How many here?
A: (Immediately.) Four.
M: (Waves her hand over both collections.) How many altogether?
A: (Looks at the desk for three seconds.) Eight.
M: (Removes the screen.)
A: (Moves one collection adjacent to the other and begins to count while pointing at each counter in turn.) One, two. (Moves a counter which is on top of another counter and then restarts her count, pointing at each counter in turn.) One, two . . . eight.
M: (Places out seven blue counters and screens them.) This time Amy there are seven under there. (Places out five red counters and does not screen them.) And five there.
A: (Immediately.) Umm – six!
M: (Points to the screened collection.) How many under here?
A: (Looks at the screen for seven seconds.) Eight.
M: Seven.
A: Seven. (After 13 seconds.) Six!
M: (Removes the screen.)
A: (Moves one collection adjacent to the other and then points at each counter in turn.) One, two . . . twelve.

Discussion of Video Excerpt 1.1

In the first task Amy answers quickly 'five' and then 'eight'. She does not appear to have a strategy involving counting. When Mary removes the screen Amy correctly counts the seven counters. In the second task Amy looks at the unscreened counters for five seconds and then answers 'one'. Mary reposes the task and Amy on this occasion answers 'eight' but no counting strategy is apparent. It seems that Amy recalls that 4 + 4 make 8 and hence is able to answer correctly on this occasion. On the third task Amy again does not have a counting strategy and her answers seem to be no more than guesses. When the screen is removed Amy seems to be immediately aware of what she is expected to do. She pushes the two collections together and correctly counts the 12 counters. Amy's act of pushing all the counters together seems to be of cognitive significance for her. It seems that, from her point of view, it now makes sense to count a collection whereas, when the counters were in two collections, regarding all of the counters as a collection, that is including the screened and unscreened counters, did not make sense. In summary, Amy does not have a strategy for solving additive tasks involving two collections, one of which is screened. This is characteristic of children classified as Stage 1: Perceptual Counting.

Video Excerpt 1.2: Heather and William

H: (Places out three red counters and screens them.) Three red counters William. I'm going to put them under there. (Places out two blue counters and screens them.) Two blue counters and I'm going to put them under there. How many counters is that altogether?

W: (Immediately.) Four.

H: Would you like to look and check?

W: (Raises screen and points to three counters in turn.) One, two, three. (Raises the other screen and points to two counters in turn.) Four, five!

H: Were you right?

W: (Shakes his head indicating that he was not correct.)

H: We'll try another one. I'll make it five red counters this time. (Places out two more red counters and screens them.) And four blue counters. (Places out two more blue counters and screens them.) How many does that make altogether?

W: (Immediately.) Eleven.

H: Eleven. How did you work that out?

W: I just knew.

H: (Removes both screens.) Would you like to check and see?

W: (Points to the nine counters in turn.) One, two . . . nine.

Heather then presented a similar task involving a screened collection of nine red counters and a screened collection of six blue counters. William immediately answered 'forty-one'.

Discussion of Video Excerpt 1.2:

Like Amy, William does not seem to have a counting strategy. Rather, on each of the three tasks he seems to immediately guess. When questioned about his response to the second task William did not seem to reflect on his strategy. His statement 'I just knew' seemed mostly motivated by a desire to say something to satisfy the teacher. It is not uncommon for children to respond in this way when questioned about their strategy, and in such situations it may be unproductive to continue to question the child. Close observation is often more informative than engaging the child in a discussion about their solution. In the previous protocol the tasks presented to Amy involved a screened and an unscreened collection, whereas the tasks presented to William involved two screened collections. Nevertheless, William, like Amy, does not count to find how many in all and seems to have no strategy other than guessing. When the counters are unscreened, William, like Amy, can count to find how many in all. This is typical of Stage 1: Perceptual Counting.

Stage 2: Figurative Counting

Children at Stage 2 solve additive tasks involving two collections, one or both of which may be screened, and in doing so count from one rather than count-on. Thus their counting involves what adults might regard as redundant activity. For example, in solving an additive task involving a screened collection of eight counters and a screened collection of four counters, the child typically begins by counting from one to eight rather than merely counting-on from eight.

Children at Stage 2 have been observed to use one or more of three types of counting, that is figural, motor or verbal. Alternatively, one could say the child counts figural, motor or verbal unit items (as discussed earlier in this chapter). Typically these types of counting arise when the child is counting the second, screened collection. In the case of figural unit items, visualized items (e.g. counters) are regarded as being significant for the child when counting. Thus in solving the above task, the child may be observed to be apparently visualizing a collection of four counters. In the case of motor unit items, movements (e.g. sequentially raising fingers) are regarded as significant because the child utters the corresponding number word after making each movement. Finally, in the case of verbal unit items, the uttered number words are regarded as significant. For example, in solving the above task the child will use double counting. Thus after counting from one to eight, the child may say 'one more is nine', etc. and thereby keep track of the four counters in the second screened collection.

The label of 'figurative' is applied collectively to figural, motor and verbal counting because each involves counting based on re-presentation (like a mental replay) of sensory-motor material, rather than direct perception of sensory-motor material which occurs at Stage 1. Figural is regarded as the least advanced of these and verbal is regarded as the most advanced, and advancement from figural to motor and motor to verbal involve progressively less dependence on re-presented sensory material. Thus the child whose most advanced strategy involves counting figural unit items is referred to as 'early

Stage 2' and the child whose most advanced strategy involves counting verbal unit items is referred to as 'late Stage 2'.

Video Excerpt 2.1: Jane and Shirley

The following video excerpt is taken from an MR teaching session.

J: (Briefly displays and then screens three counters. Then screens two counters.) And two here. How many have I got altogether? Three and two?

S: (Looks at the screen covering three counters and makes three points in co-ordination with counting.) One, two, three (turns to the other screen and make two points in co-ordination with counting), four, five.

J: (Removes both screens.) Show me.

S: (Points at each counter in turn.) One, two, three – four, five.

J: Right. What about if I put five here (screens five counters) and three here? (Screens three counters.)

S: (Looks at the screen covering three counters and makes three points in co-ordination with counting.) One, two, three (looks at the other screen and again co-ordinates a point with each number word), four, five, six, seven (pauses and looks up), eight!

J: (Removes both screens.) Show me.

S: (Points at each counter in turn.) One, two, three – four, five, six, seven, eight!

J: What about if I put ten here (screens ten counters) and three here (screens three counters).

S: (Looks at the screen covering three counters and makes three points in co-ordination with counting.) One, two, three (looks at the other screen and again co-ordinates a point with each number word) four, five, six, seven, eight, nine (pauses and looks up) – ten – eleven, twelve?

J: Have another think. (Places her hand on the screen covering ten counters.) Start with this side. How many here?

S: Ten.

J: Right. Start with this side.

S: (Looking up) One, two, three, four (in co-ordination with four points), five, six (looks at the screen and appears to feel the counters).

J: (Interrupting.) No, don't feel them. How many are here?

S: (Places left hand on the screen covering ten counters.) Ten there – .

J: Alright and three there.

S: (Places right hand on other screen.) Three there. (Looks at the screen covering ten counters and co-ordinates a point with each number word.) One, two, three, four, five, six (looks at the second screen) seven – .

J: (Interrupting) No, ten here (points to the screen).

S: Ten, three (places a hand on each screen).

J: Start at ten and count these ones on (points to each screen in turn).

S: (Looks at the screen covering ten counters and then touches the screen four times in co-ordination with counting). One, two, three, four.

J: (Interrupting) No, don't touch them. We know how many are there. How many are there? (Removes the screen.) You count them.

S: (Points to each counter in turn.) One, two . . . ten.

J: (Rescreens the counters.) Now do we have to count them again? How many are there?

S: Ten.

J: Now let's just say ten.

J: (Points to the screen covering three counters.)

S: Three!

J: (Points to the screen covering ten counters.) Ten – . (Points to the screen covering three counters.)

S: Three.

J: (Points to the screen covering ten counters.) Ten —. How many altogether? (Points again to the screen covering ten counters.) Ten – .

S: (Looks at Jane and then looks at the screen covering ten counters and makes ten points in co-ordination with counting.) One, two . . . ten (looks at the second screen and continues to make points in co-ordination with counting), eleven, twelve, thirteen!

Discussion of Video Excerpt 2.1

In the first task (3 and 2) Shirley counts aloud from one and keeps track of the second collection (i.e. two counters). In the second task (5 and 3) Shirley counts from one, first counting the collection of three counters and then the collection five. Thus her solution involves keeping track of five counts. Because Shirley solves tasks involving screened collections and, in doing so, counts from one she is classified as Stage 2: Figurative Counting. Shirley's strategy seems to involve visualizing, that is, figural counting or counting figural unit items. She seems to visualize the second collection to keep track of the items to be counted. Although her strategy involves movements, that is, pointing at the counters, her visualizing seems to be the most significant aspect of her counting. In the last task (10 and 3) we see that Shirley seems necessarily to have to count from 'one' and doing so provides meaning to 'ten' for Shirley. This is typical of children at Stage 2. As in the earlier tasks, Shirley's strategy seems to involve visualizing the second collection when continuing after counting to 'ten'.

Video Excerpt 2.2: Molly and Tom

M: (Places out five red counters and screens them and then places out four blue counters and screens them.) Now if I've got five counters there Tom and I cover them up and four counters here and I cover them up, how many counters would I have altogether there?

T: (Smiles and shifts in his seat.) These are the hard ones. (Thinks for three seconds.) Umm.

M: (Nods and points at each collection in turn.) Five and four?

T: (Looks momentarily at the screens and then looks up and to his right. Then counts subvocally for seven seconds.) Nine!

M: Why do you think it's nine?

T: Because I counted through them.

M: Did you? How did you count? Could you just tell me?

T: I went one, two, three, four, five (points at the screen covering five counters and then looks at the second screen), and then one, two, three, four. (Pauses.) So it's seven. I can tell that's seven – .

M: (M interrupts Tom's thinking and removes the screens.) Umm.

T: So I went – (counts subvocally from one to nine in co-ordination with moving each counter in turn). Yes!

M: (Places out seven red counters and screens them and then places out five blue counters and screens them.) Seven red ones and five blue ones. Seven and five. How many would that be altogether?

T: (Looks at the screen covering seven red counters and counts subvocally. Then looks at the second screen and continues to count subvocally.) Twelve!

M: (Removes the screens.) Want to check to see if you are right?

T: (Moves each counter in co-ordination with counting.) One, two . . . twelve!

Discussion of Video Excerpt 2.2

In each of the two tasks Tom's strategy is to count subvocally. Nevertheless it is reasonably apparent that he is counting from 'one' and this is confirmed in his explanation of his solution to the first task. In both tasks, when continuing after counting the first collection Tom seems to focus on the number words themselves. Thus, in the first task, for example, although he does not explicitly double count, he seems to focus on the words from 'six' to 'nine' in order to keep track of making four counts, rather than visualize as in the case of Shirley. As discussed above this is referred to as verbal counting or counting verbal unit items.

Stage 3: Initial Number Sequence

As described in Chapter 2, children at Stage 3 use counting-on to solve additive and Missing Addend tasks and may also use counting-down-from to solve Removed Items tasks. When solving an additive task such as 8 and 4, for example, presented as two screened collections, the child seems to be aware that, when counting-on, the number word 'eight' signifies the act of having counted the first collection from 'one' to 'eight'.

Video Excerpt 3.1: Julie and Tania

J: I've got five under there (points to a screen), and four under there (points to a second screen).

T: (Counts subvocally in co-ordination with pointing in turn at four fingers on her left hand.) Nine.

J: How did you work that out?

T: Counted on my fingers.

J: What numbers did you count?

T: (Points to her one finger.) Six – (pauses), five, six, seven, eight, nine. (Co-ordinates the last four number words with pointing to each finger in turn.)

J: I've got nine under there and six under there. How many altogether?

T: Nine, ten . . . fifteen (points in turn at the five fingers on her left hand and one finger on her right hand).

Discussion of Video Excerpt 3.1

Tania's strategy for solving these tasks involves counting-on and using her fingers to keep track of the number of her counts, that is, when counting the second collection. In the first task, for example, she does not raise her four fingers prior to commencing to count, that is, it is not necessary for her to raise four fingers in advance in order to keep track of counting-on. Rather, her strategy involves recognizing when she has raised four fingers to keep track of the second collection. In the second task, in similar vein, Tania knows when she has raised six fingers to keep track. Her counting-on strategy includes a quite facile (i.e. skilful) use of finger patterns.

Video Excerpt 3.2: Jane and Shirley
The following video excerpt is taken from an MR teaching session.

J: (Points to a screen and then covers four counters with a second screen.) Twelve, and I've got four more under here?

S: (Places her hand on the first screen and looks ahead.) Twelve. (Moves her hand to the second screen. After three seconds during which time she moves her fingers over the second screen.) Sixteen!

J: Alright. Maybe we can just pretend. (Places a screen on the desk.) If I say, under here I've got – I'm pretending there's twenty-four. Twenty-four (places out and screens three counters), and three more?

S: Twenty-four (points to the second screen and answers almost immediately), twenty-seven.

J: Great work. (Places out a screen.) Let's pretend there's forty-five under here. Forty-five (places out a screen covering four counters), and four more.

S: (Places her hand on the first screen.) Forty-five (moves her hand over the second screen and counts subvocally), forty-nine!

J: (Places out a screen.) Let's pretend there's fifty-eight under here. Fifty-eight (places out a screen covering three counters), and three more.

S: (Places her hand on the first screen. Then moves her hand to the second screen and counts subvocally while moving her fingers.) Sixty-two!

J: No, have a think. (Places her hand on the first screen) fifty-eight – (moves her hand to the second screen).

S: (Looks at the second screen for two seconds.) Sixty-one.

J: (Places her hand on the first screen.) What about if I've got eighty-two under there? (Briefly displays and then screens five counters.) Eighty-two and five more?

S: (Looks at the second screen momentarily and then looks up and to her left. Counts subvocally for six seconds.) Eighty-seven.

Discussion of Video Excerpt 3.2
In this excerpt Shirley solves five additive tasks – 12 and 4, 24 and 3,

45 and 4, 58 and 3, 82 and 5 – by counting-on. One can hypothesize about the means by which Shirley keeps track of the second collection. Shirley does not appear to explicitly double count. Nevertheless she appears to focus on her number words when counting-on. A plausible explanation is that Shirley uses patterns for counting-on a given number of counts and that these patterns are temporal sequences of counts that she can apply irrespective of the particular number words. Prior to commencing her count, Shirley seems to anticipate that she can count-on the given number of counts. In summary, Shirley has a facile and spontaneous counting-on strategy which is indicative of a child at Stage 3: Initial Number Sequence.

Stage 4: Intermediate Number Sequence

As described in Chapter 2, Stage 4 is characterized by an ability to use counting-down-to to solve Missing Subtrahend tasks. For example, children at Stage 4 might solve a task involving screened collections such as – 'I have 12 counters and I remove some and now there are 8. How many did I remove?' When commencing to count-down-to on this task, these children seem to be simultaneously aware of the larger collection of 12 counters and the collection of 8 counters contained within the larger collection. This counting strategy is regarded as cognitively more advanced than those used at Stage 3.

Video Excerpt 4.1: Libby and Kelley

L: (Places out '10 – 7 =', using plastic digits and signs.) This time, ten take seven away?

K: Ten. (Raises ten fingers directly in front of her. Looks at her right hand and then her left. Lowers two fingers on her left hand and then all five on her right. Picks up the plastic digit for '3' and places it beside the equals sign.)

L: Right. Okay, now try this one. (Places out '16 – 12 =') Sixteen take twelve away?

K: (After 20 seconds, raises her thumb and index finger. Then lowers both her thumb and index finger.) Umm fifteen (raises her thumb and then pauses), fourteen, thirteen (in co-ordination with raising two fingers in turn. Pauses, then raises her third finger and utters uncertainly), twelve. (Looks at her fingers, then simultaneously raises her little finger and lowers her thumb.) Four!

Discussion of Video Excerpt 4.1

In the first task, 10 – 7, presented with plastic numerals, Kelley uses a strategy that we might suppose is convenient for her. She simultaneously raises 10 fingers and then looks carefully at her fingers and after a little while lowers 2 fingers on her left hand and then the 5 fingers on her right hand. A plausible explanation is that, at this point she has established a finger pattern that stands for 7 for her, that is for the 7 being taken away. She immediately knows that now she has 3 fingers remaining, that is, she recognizes a finger pattern for three and it is not necessary for her to count from one. In summary, Kelley knows the patterns for 10 and 3, and she builds a pattern for 7 by lowering two fingers on one hand and then five on the other. Kelley's strategy on this task involves facile use of finger patterns. Thus her solution in the first task does not provide an indication of whether she might use advanced counting strategies in some tasks.

The second task involves 16 – 12 and is presented with plastic numerals. It seems reasonable to suggest that Kelley cannot use finger patterns on this task because she cannot readily make a pattern to signify 16. In other words, 16 is 'beyond the finger range' in terms of signifying numbers in the same way as done in the task of 10 – 7. Kelley seems to spend around 20 seconds focusing on trying to solve the problem after which she seems to suddenly become aware of a strategy that she can use. Kelley uses a counting-down-to strategy to solve the task. She begins at 16 and then keeps track of the number of counts until she gets to 12 and stops, and she uses her fingers on her right hand to keep track. A plausible explanation is that, prior to beginning to count down, Kelley was aware of the 12 as being a part of the 16. She was aware of 12 as a whole, or as a unit within the larger unit of 16. It is this kind of thinking that is the hallmark of Stage 4. She is able to conceptualize the smaller unit within the larger unit prior to commencing her count. It is also interesting to see that she raises her thumb and 3 fingers and then deftly switches the pattern by lowering her thumb and raising her little finger. She then recognizes immediately her finger pattern for 4. She does not have to count from 'one' to 'four'. In summary, Kelley uses counting-down-to and in doing so uses her fingers to keep track of four counts. For this reason Kelley is classified as Stage 4: the Intermediate Number Sequence.

Video Excerpt 4.2: Terry and Sarah

T: There's eight there, okay? (Places eight counters under a screen.) I'm taking some away (reaches under the screen and removes two counters without displaying them), and I've got six left (momentarily displays the remaining six counters). How many did I take away?

S: (Immediately.) Two.

T: How did you do that so quickly?

S: (Shrugging her shoulders.) I don't know.

T: Twelve, okay? There's twelve there this time. (Places twelve counters under a screen.) I am going to take some away (reaches under the screen and removes three counters without displaying them), and there are nine left (momentarily displays the remaining nine counters).

S: (Sequentially raises three fingers.) Three?

T: Okay, now what numbers were you saying to yourself to get those three?

S: I was saying twelve, and I took away some and then I counted to nine, so I went, twelve, eleven, ten (in co-ordination with raising three fingers), and that was nine (moves her fourth finger), so I put that down and then I worked it out.

Discussion of Video Excerpt 4.2

In the first task, Terry's questioning of Sarah about her strategy seems most appropriate, in that she does not continue questioning after Sarah says 'I don't know'. A reasonable explanation of this is that Sarah knows the answer to 8 − 6 and does not use a strategy to obtain the answer. Continuing to question a child about their strategy in this kind of situation can be somewhat disconcerting for the child. The second task is apparently more challenging for Sarah. In her explanation it becomes apparent that Sarah indeed has counted backwards. She has used a counting-down-to strategy to solve this Missing Subtrahend task. She raised 3 fingers to keep track of counting down. After completing her counting down, she recognizes the finger-pattern for 3. Terry once again very skilfully questions without leading, and without presupposition or presumption, and Sarah's strategy unfolds. This is another excellent example of a count-down-to strategy that is characteristic of Stage 4.

Stage 5: Facile Number Sequence

As described in Chapter 2, Stage 5 is characterized by the use of a range of strategies that involves procedures other than counting by ones. A Stage 5 strategy may incorporate one of the advanced counting-by-ones strategies but, importantly, will also incorporate one or more procedures that differ from counting-by-ones.

Video Excerpt 5.1: Robin and Allan

R: (Places 12 counters under a screen.) There were twelve counters and I took away some (removes and screens three counters), and I have nine left. How many did I take away?

A: (Looks at Robin) Three.

R: How did you work that out?

A: Nine plus three is twelve, and then you take away, it's nine.

R: (Places 15 counters under a screen and then removes and screens four counters.) This time I had fifteen counters, I took some away and I have eleven left. Fifteen, took some away and I've got eleven left.

A: (Looks ahead for nine seconds.) Four!

R: Tell me how you did that one.

A: Umm, you had fifteen and took some away to make eleven because you just take away four, 'cause if you took away five it would be ten and you just plus it on.

R: (Places counters under a screen.) What if I start off with fifteen under there (removes, displays and then screens three counters), take three out, how many are left under there?

A: Twelve.

R: Hmm, how did you do that one?

A: Because five take away three is two, and then you just, 'cause there was fifteen so you just take away three and it's twelve.

Discussion of Video Excerpt 5.1

Allan shows a good number of non-count-by-ones strategies on these tasks. In the case of the first task – 12 take-away some, now I have 9, how many did I take away – it becomes apparent in Allan's explanation that he worked this Missing Subtrahend task out by thinking of the addition '9 and 3 are 12'. This is a very advanced strategy for a 6-year-old and is an excellent example of a non-count-by-ones strategy. Strategies such as this are commonly referred to as thinking strategies for the basic facts, that is, using addition to work out subtraction, or exploiting knowledge that subtraction and addition are inverse operations. Allan's solution of the second task involves knowledge of the tens and ones structure of the number 15. Allan realizes that 15 is 10 and 5. Again this is very advanced for a 6-year-old and not typical of children lower than Stage 5. Allan also uses what is commonly referred to as a compensation strategy – if 5 are taken from 15 the answer is 10, thus, if the answer is 11, only 4 are taken away. These strategies are very advanced and are referred to as non-count-by-ones strategies.

In the final task in this excerpt, 15 take away 3, Allan in explanation indicates that he has worked the task out by thinking of 5 take away 3. As with the above strategies this is an example of a non-count-by-ones strategy. He seems to be aware of a correspondence of the relationship between 5 and 15 on the one hand with the relationship between 2 and 12 on the other hand, that is, in both cases the second number is 10 more than the first. Given the problem of the names of these numbers, for example 'twelve', which does not give any clue of the relationship between 2 and 12, it seems plausible to suggest that Allan is thinking in terms of written symbols perhaps even written symbols arranged in columns. This corresponds with how we might expect an advanced child, or a child beyond Year 1, to work such a subtraction. Whatever the precise nature of Allan's thinking, it is quite advanced. In Allan's solutions we see strategies well beyond counting-by-ones. His strategies, considered across all of these tasks, are characteristic of Stage 5: the Facile Number Sequence, where non-count-by-ones strategies are used spontaneously.

Video Excerpt 5.2: Kathryn and Loretta

K: If we have five under there (places five counters under a screen) and four under there (places four counters under a second screen), how many would we have?

L: (Immediately.) Five and four more is nine.

K: And how do you know that?

L: Well, five and three more is eight and so one more is nine.

Discussion of Video Excerpt 5.2

Loretta, in explanation, reveals a strategy where 5 plus 4 is worked out from 5 plus 3. This kind of strategy, that is, using a known fact to work out an unknown and making an appropriate adjustment – one more in this case – is well known and is referred to as a 'thinking strategy' for the basic facts. Because Loretta uses a strategy that has features other than counting-by-ones she is classified as Stage 5: Facile Number Sequence.

Summary

The model of the Stages of Early Arithmetical Learning provides a means of understanding the progression of children's early number learning from perceptual counting strategies in which children are reliant on seeing materials to the point were children have a relatively sophisticated knowledge of addition and subtraction, in the range 1 to 100 and beyond. Children at the Perceptual Stage (Stage 1) can solve problems involving visible items, whereas children at the Figurative Stage (Stage 2) can solve problems involving hidden items but count from one when doing so. Children at the stage of the Initial Number Sequence (Stage 3) use counting-on to solve additive and/or Missing Addend tasks, and may use counting-down-from to solve Removed Items tasks, while children at the stage of the Intermediate Number Sequence (Stage 4) use counting-down-to to solve Missing Subtrahend tasks. Finally, children at the stage of the Facile Number Sequence (Stage 5) use a range of strategies other than counting-by-ones to solve additive and subtractive tasks. (See Table 2.2 on p. 26).

5

Identifying the Stages of Early Arithmetical Learning

In this chapter we present scenarios similar to the examples in Chapter 4 and challenge you to determine the stage of SEAL for each example. The chapter provides the answer for each example and an explanation of why each child is placed at a particular stage.

Analysis of Mathematics Recovery assessments involves a good deal of learning on the part of teachers. This learning is best undertaken through practice, reflection and discussion, and this chapter introduces the reader to this process. Twelve scenarios of children's problem-solving activity in early number are presented. These scenarios are based on actual assessments by MR teachers, and focus specifically on Task Groups 8 and 9 of Assessment A, that is, additive and subtractive tasks. The exercise for the reader is to study each scenario carefully in order to determine the child's stage in terms of the SEAL model. This exercise serves several purposes. As well as providing important practice for the reader in analysing children's problem-solving activity, it provides insights into the ways in which teachers present tasks and interact with children during MR assessment, and exemplifies the ways children respond to the assessment tasks.

Readers should bear in mind that MR assessment aims to determine the most advanced strategy available to the child. This is equally important in the administration of the assessment interview and its analysis. The child's use of this strategy should be spontaneous, that is, unassisted either directly or indirectly by the teacher. As a general rule the child should use the strategy in solving several tasks, rather than only the introductory task, for example. Each of the 12 scenarios in this chapter has been selected because, in the view of the authors it provides a reasonably clear-cut example of children's problem-solving at a given stage. Readers should aim to carefully identify each strategy used by the child and then determine the most advanced strategy available to the child, before moving on to the detailed discussion and the stage identification that follow each scenario.

Scenarios of Children's Early Number Problem-Solving Activity

Collectively these 12 scenarios exemplify all six stages of SEAL. Each of the stages is exemplified by two scenarios.

Scenario 1: Heather and Tina

Tina was presented with the following three additive tasks: 3 and 2, 5 and 4, and 9 and 6, involving two screened collections. She solved each of these on her first attempt.

H: (Briefly displays and then screens three blue counters and simi-larly two red counters.) Do you know how many there are altogether?

T: Umm. (Looks at the screen covering three counters for six sec-onds.) Five!

H: How did you work that out?

T: Umm, I said – umm, umm I read it in my mind and I – and it went three and then I counted the rest and it worked out to five.

H: (Presents the second task of 5 and 4.) Five and four more?

T: (Looks ahead for four seconds then looks to the right for three seconds.) Nine!

H: Hmm. What did you do that time?

T: I just counted them all.

H: Can you tell me what numbers you counted?

T: Hmm, I counted one, two . . . nine.

H: (Presents the third task of 9 and 6.) Nine this time and six more?

T: (Looks in the direction of the screens for nine seconds.) Fifteen!

H: What did you do that time to help you?

T: Well, I did the same, like when it was – there was five there and four there (points at the screens in turn).

H: Hmm, where did you start counting from?

T: Up to nine.

H: You counted up to nine did you?

T: Hmm (nods affirmatively).

H: And then you did what?

T: Well, I said nine and then I counted the rest.

Tina was presented with four Missing Subtrahend tasks, that is, 3 to 2, 8 to 6, 12 to 9 and 6 to 4. She solved the first and last of these only. Heather modified her presentation of the last task in the fol-lowing way. After partitioning the minuend she left the known differ-ence unscreened (four counters in this case) whereas on the first three tasks, both the known difference and the missing subtrahend were screened after partitioning. Tina's solution to the last task, that is, 6 to 4, is shown in the following video excerpt:

H: (Arranges six counters into a 3 × 2 array.) Okay there are six there. Can you look away for a moment? (Removes and screens two adjacent counters from one row of three, leaving the remaining four counters unscreened.) Look back. There are only four left. How many did I take away?

T: (Looks at the four counters.) Umm – two!

H: (Unscreens the two counters.) How did you know it was two?

T: (Points to the four counters.) Because I knew there has to be two more there to make six.

Tina was presented with four Removed Items tasks, that is, 3 r 1, 10 r 2, 15 r 3 and 5 r 2. She solved the first and last of these only. Heather modified her presentation of the last task similarly to the way she modified the last Missing Subtrahend task, that is, she left the removed items (two in this case) unscreened after partitioning the minuend. For the task of 10 r 2 Tina answered 'five' and for 15 r 3 she answered 'six'. Her strategies for solving these two tasks were not apparent. Tina's solution to the task of 5 r 3 is shown in the following video excerpt:

H: (Briefly displays and then screens five counters.) I'm going to start with five this time. Okay, cover it up. (Removes two counters and leaves them unscreened.) Put my hand under and take two away. How many left?

T: Umm – three!

H: How did you know that?

T: Umm, because I knew there would be two more to make five.

Scenario 1: Heather and Tina – Solution
Tina solved the three additive tasks presented to her and the evidence suggests that she counted from one when doing so. Each of the three additive tasks involved two screened collections and it is clear that Tina did not count perceptual items (i.e. visible items) on her solutions. This suggests that Tina was at Stage 2, that is, Figurative Counting. In the case of the Missing Subtrahend tasks, Tina did not display a general strategy for solving these tasks. Solving the introductory task of '3 to 2' was not a sufficient indicator of a more advanced strategy. Similarly, in solving the task of '6 to 4' her solution seemed to depend on the four counters being unscreened. There is no indication that she

used the counting-down-to strategy. In similar vein, Tina did not use counting-down-from to solve the Removed Items tasks. She was able to solve the introductory task and her solution to the last task seemed to depend on the three counters being unscreened. Thus Tina is judged to be at Stage 2, that is, Figurative Counting.

Scenario 2: Tamara and Jack

Jack was presented with the following five additive tasks involving two screened collections: 3 and 2, 5 and 4, 9 and 6, 8 and 5 and 9 and 3. He solved each of these on his first attempt. On the first task (3 and 2) he answered 'five' quickly and when asked how he did it he said 'I just knew it was five'. The following video excerpt begins after Jack had quickly answered 'nine' to the second task (5 and 4).

T: How did you do it?

J: I just knew it was nine and – if you had five and you put up four it would be nine.

T: (Presents the third task.) Okay we've got nine and six. How many altogether?

J: (Looks up for six seconds then raises five fingers on his left hand and one on his right simultaneously). Okay six – (places his left hand on the first screen keeping his fingers raised), wait, nine – (raises his left hand then raises the second finger on his right hand), ten – (lowers the finger just raised) wait, nine – (touches each of his raised fingers in co-ordination with counting), ten, eleven, twelve, thirteen, fourteen, fifteen.

Jack solved the fourth (8 and 5) task similarly to the way he solved the third. His solution involved raising five fingers on his left hand simultaneously and then touching each finger in co-ordination with counting from nine to thirteen. On the fifth task (9 and 3) Jack quickly answered 'twelve'. On this task it seemed that Jack recalled a known fact. Jack was presented with two Missing Addend tasks, that is, 4 to 6 and 12 to 15 which he solved. On the first of these he first answered 'eleven' – seeming to misinterpret the task as the additive task of 4 and 6.

Jack was presented with the following four Missing Subtrahend tasks: 5 to 3, 10 to 6, 12 to 9 and 15 to 11. He solved each of these tasks on his first attempt. On the first task he quickly answered 'two'. Jack's solution to the second task (10 to 6) is shown in the following video excerpt.

T: And now we have six. How many did I take away?

J: How many did you have?

T: Ten.

J: (After seven seconds, raises four fingers.)

T: Okay, how did you do it?

J: Kind of – kind of thinking.

T: Tell me how you were thinking.

J: Well – (mumbles), I think it would be four.

T: (Raises the screen covering four counters.) Well you're right but I want to understand how you did that. (Raises the screen covering six counters.) We started out with ten and now we have six. Tell me how you get four.

J: (After three seconds.) I counted up.

T: Do that for me?

J: (Raises five fingers on his left hand and then points to his thumb.) Ten – I mean ten –. (Lowers his thumb and then raises his right hand above his head with his point finger extended.) Ten! (Touches each finger on his left hand in co-ordination with counting) nine, eight, seven, six.

T: Okay so you really counted down didn't you?

J: Hmm-mm (affirmatively).

In solving the third task (12 to 9) Jack touched three fingers in co-ordination with counting subvocally. In explaining his solution he said 'I counted down'. In explaining his solution to the fourth task (15 to 11) Jack again said 'I counted down'.

Jack was presented with the following four Removed Items tasks: 3 r 1, 10 r 2, 15 r 3, 27 r 4. He solved each of these tasks on his first attempt. His strategies typically involved subvocal counting without moving his fingers.

Scenario 2: Tamara and Jack – Solution

Jack used a range of advanced strategies involving counting-by-ones to solve additive and subtractive tasks. He used counting-up-from to solve all but one of the additive tasks. He solved two Missing Addend tasks although he may have initially misinterpreted the first. Finally, Jack used counting-down-to to solve Missing Subtrahend tasks. Thus Jack was at least at Stage 4. On three of the additive tasks, that is, 3 and 2, 5 and 4, and 9 and 3, Jack answered quickly. In doing so Jack provided some indication that his strategies on these tasks did not involve counting-by-ones. His explanation of his solution to the second of these (5 and 4) suggests an awareness of the finger pattern for nine consisting of five fingers on one hand and four on the other. Overall, his solutions do not constitute sufficient evidence that he is at Stage 5. His solutions could be attributed to addition facts that he knows, for example $3 + 2 = 5$, or can work out quickly, for example $5 + 4 = 9$. Beyond this there is little indication that Jack can use a range of non-count-by-ones strategies. Thus Jack is judged to be at Stage 4, that is, Intermediate Number Sequence.

Scenario 3: Wendy and Bill

Bill was presented with three additive tasks involving two screened collections, that is, 5 and 4, 9 and 6, and 8 and 5. On the first task Bill immediately answered 'nine' and explained his answer as follows: 'Because five plus five is ten, and then four plus five must be nine, because it's missing one more from five.' On the second task Bill answered 'fifteen' after 15 seconds. In explaining his answer he said 'well three plus three is six and then there's three more so that makes nine and then there's another three and then there's another three.' The following video excerpt continues after Wendy presented the additive task of 8 and 5 with two screened collections.

W: What would it be if it was eight and five more?
B: (After six seconds.) Thirteen!
W: Yes. How did you do that?
B: Well, it had to be thirteen because there wasn't ten and if there was ten it would be fifteen.

Following this Bill solved two Missing Addend tasks, that is, 6 to 10 and 12 to 15. In explaining his solution of 12 to 15 he indicated that he had used 10 and $5 = 15$. Following this Bill solved the two Missing Subtrahend tasks of 10 to 6 and 12 to 9 and answered 'three' to the task of 15 to 11. In explaining his solution to 12 to 15 he said 'I can count by threes and I can count back by threes.' The following video excerpt shows Bill's solution to 10 to 6.

W: Look back! There were ten. I've taken some away and now there's only six left. How many did I take away?
B: (Immediately.) Three, I mean four!
W: Why four? How did you know that?
B: Because six plus four is ten and then if I swap it around the other way, it's that way.

Bill solved the Removed Items tasks of 10 r 2, 15 r 3, 17 r 14 and 27 r 4. On the second of these Bill explained his answer by saying 'because it's only three more from twelve to get to fifteen.' On the task of 17 r 14 Bill answered 'four'. His method of solution was not apparent. Bill's solution to 27 r 4 is shown in the following video excerpt.

W: Twenty-seven and I'm taking out four. What's left?
B: (Looks ahead for 15 seconds.) Twenty-three!
W: Right. How did you know twenty-three?
B: Counted backwards.

Scenario 3: Wendy and Bill – Solution
Bill used a range of non-count-by-ones strategies to solve additive and subtractive tasks. He used the known fact of 5 + 5 to solve 5 and 4 and similarly 10 + 5 to solve 8 and 5. In solving 9 and 6 he seemed to be able to regard nine as three threes and six as two threes. He used the known addition fact of 6 + 4 = 10 to work out the Missing Subtrahend task of '10 to 6'. In the final example Bill used counting-down-from to solve a Removed Items task. Thus in some cases Bill might use a counting strategy. Nevertheless he has a range of robust non-count-by-ones strategies and was clearly at Stage 5, that is, Facile Number Sequence.

Scenario 4: Renae and Carol
R: (Briefly displays and then screens three blue counters.) I'm going to put three blue counters under this screen. (Briefly displays and then screens two red counters.) And I'm going to put two over here. Can you tell me how many I've got altogether?
C: (Places her hands on the screen covering three blue counters.) Three in this one. (Points to the other screen.) Two in that one. Let me see. (Counts subvocally while first placing her hands and head on the first screen and then looking up.) Four?
R: Have a look and see. (Raises the screens.) Were you right?
C: (Touches the blue counters.) Umm yep!
R: Count them for me.
C: (Points to the two red counters.) Two (points to one blue counter), three. (Starts again, pointing to each blue counter in turn.) One, two, three!
R: How many altogether? (Moves the two red counters to a position adjacent to the three blue counters.)
C: (Points to each counter in turn.) One, two, three, four, five!

Renae then posed an addition task involving five red counters that were screened and two blue counters that were unscreened.

C: (Points at the screen in co-ordination with counting subvocally from 'one' to 'four'. Starts again counting quietly in co-ordination with pointing at the screen.) One – (attempts to feel the counters), one, two, three, four.

R: There's five under there.

C: (Points at the screen in co-ordination with counting.) One, two, three, four, five!

R: (Points to the two unscreened counters.) And? (Waves her hand over the screen and the two unscreened counters.) Altogether, five – .

C: (Raises her hands.) That makes ten!

R: (Removes the screen.) What if we take that away. How many now?

C: (Moves the two red counters adjacent to the blue counters and then points to each counter in turn.) One, two . . . seven!

Renae then placed out thirteen blue counters and asked Carol to count them. Carol made three unsuccessful attempts to count these. First, she counted ten of the counters using pointing actions and stopped appearing to lose track. She then started again counting 'one, two . . . twelve, fifteen, fourteen'. Thus making a co-ordination error, that is, fourteen counts rather than thirteen, and a number word sequence error. Renae then arranged the counters in a line and asked Carol to count them again. On this occasion she again pointed to the counters in turn making three co-ordination errors, that is, making 16 points instead of 13. She concluded her count with 'fourteen, eighteen, ninety'.

Scenario 4: Renae and Carol – Solution
Carol made two types of errors when attempting to count the collection of 13 counters. First, she makes a co-ordination error on each of her two attempts. On her first attempt she made 14 counts rather than 13 and on her second attempt she made 16 counts. Secondly, Carol made a number word sequence error on each of her two attempts. For these reasons Carol is judged to be at Stage 0, that is, Emergent Counting.

Scenario 5: Terry and Belinda
T: (Briefly displays and then screens three green counters.) Here's three counters. I'm going to cover them up. (Briefly displays and then screens two white counters.) Here's two more counters. How many counters altogether?

B: (Immediately.) Ten.

T: How did you get ten?

B: Because there's three under there (points to first screen) and two under there (points to the second screen.)

Terry restated the task several times, finally removing the screen covering the three counters but Belinda did not attempt to count and did not solve the task. The next task involved five green counters which were unscreened and two white counters which were screened. After two seconds Belinda said ' equals um – ten!' Again Terry restated the task several times finally removing the second screen so that both collections were unscreened, and as before, Belinda did not attempt to count and answered incorrectly each time. Her answers appeared to be little more than guesses. Terry then directed Belinda's attention to each collection in turn.

T: (Traces around the five green counters.) How many are here?

B: (Looks at the five counters and counts subvocally.) Five!

T: (Traces around the two green counters,) And how many are there?

B: (Immediately.) Two.

T: (Nods and then pauses.) So how many does that make altogether?

B: (Looks at the two green counters.) Two.

Terry restated the task several times but Belinda did not correctly solve the task. On one occasion she appeared to count subvocally but did not look at the counters when doing so. She answered 'eleven'. Soon after this Terry placed 13 green counters on the desk.

T: How many counters are there altogether? And you can count them. Can you count them to see how many there are?

B: (Pointing at each counter in turn.) One, two . . . thirteen. Thirteen!

T: There's thirteen there. Okay. Alright I'm going to give you some more now. (Adds five green counters making a collection of eighteen.) Now I've given you some more counters Belinda. How many counters are there now?

B: Count 'em?

T: Umm.

B: (Counts quickly, pointing at each counter in turn) One, two . . . seventeen (omits one counter). Seventeen!

After a brief discussion Belinda counted the counters again but more slowly on this occasion and answered 'eighteen!'

Scenario 5: Terry and Belinda – Solution

Belinda correctly counted a collection of 13 counters. On her first attempt to count a collection of 18 counters Belinda answered 17 and on her second attempt correctly answered 18. This indicates that Belinda was at least at Stage 1. Belinda was unable to solve tasks involving two screened collections, for example she did not attempt to count from one or count-on to solve these tasks. This indicates that Belinda was not at Stage 2. Thus Belinda was at Stage 1, that is, Perceptual Counting. On each of the two tasks involving two screened collections, when Belinda did not solve the task, Terry removed the screens and asked Belinda how many counters in all. Of interest is that in these cases Belinda also did not use counting. She did not seem to conceive of the two collections as being reorganized into one collection that could be counted. This is typical of some children at Stage 1, and also some children at Stage 0.

Scenario 6: Terry and John

T: (Places out five counters in a row.) How many counters are there?

J: (Looks at the counters.) Three.

T: Count them.

J: (Counts slowly pointing at each counter in turn.) One, two, three, four, five.

T: So how many counters are there?

J: Five.

T: Okay, I'm going to cover up that. (Places a screen on the five counters.) You have to remember there are five. And I'm going to give you two more (places out two counters), how many would we have now altogether?

J: (Looks at the two counters.) Two.

T: (Points to the two counters.) There's two there isn't there? But what if I went (raises the screen and waves her hand over the seven counters), how many are there altogether now?

J: Five. That one and that one and that one (saying 'that one' three times while pointing in turn at the two counters) and that one and that one and that one and that one and that one (points to each of the five counters in turn).

T: Umm, okay (waves her hand over the counters). Altogether there are how many?

J: (Immediately.) Six.

T: Have you got a way of checking that John? How would you check to see if six is how many there are?

J: One, two ... five (points to each of the five counters in turn). One, two (points to each of the two counters in turn).

Following this Terry moved all of the counters together and asked John to count them. In doing so he pointed at the counters in turn but made only six points rather than seven, that is, he incorrectly co-ordinated his points with the counters. Following this John correctly counted eight counters arranged in two rows of four but made co-ordination errors when attempting to count seven, thirteen and eight-een counters. On these tasks John's counting included several number word sequence errors in the teens, for example he omitted 'thirteen' and 'seventeen'.

Scenario 6: Terry and John – Solution
On two occasions John made a co-ordination error when attempting to count seven counters. He also made co-ordination errors when attempting to count 13 and 18 counters. John also made number word sequence errors in the teens when attempting to count collections of counters. This indicates that John was at Stage 0, the Emergent Stage. When asked to count the counters which were arranged in a collec-tion of five and a collection of two, John counted each collection sep-arately. As in the case of Belinda in Scenario 5, John did not seem to be able to regard the counters as being reorganized into one collec-tion which could be counted.

Scenario 7: Tanya and Kelly
Kelly was presented with the following additive tasks involving two screened collections: 3 and 2, 5 and 4, 9 and 6, 8 and 5, and 9 and 3. She solved one task (3 and 2) on her first attempt, three on her sec-ond attempt and answered 'sixteen' to the task of 9 and 6. In attempt-ing to solve these tasks Kelly did not count aloud or subvocally – no lip movements were apparent. She typically looked ahead with her hands under the desk. Her solution to one task (8 and 5) is described in the following video excerpt.

T: (Briefly displays and then screens the first collection.) This time there are eight green counters (briefly displays and then screens the second collection) and five yellow counters. How many coun-ters altogether?

K: (Looks ahead with both hands under the desk for ten seconds.) Fifteen!

T: There's eight under there (briefly displays the first collection) and five under there (briefly displays the second collection).

K: (Looks ahead with hands under the desk for 11 seconds.) Thirteen!

Kelly was presented with the following five Missing Subtrahend tasks: 5 to 3, 6 to 4, 10 to 6, 12 to 9, and 15 to 11. She was typically unsuccessful on these tasks. The following video excerpt shows her attempt at solving the last of these tasks.

T: (Places out 15 counters and asks Kelly to look away. Screens four of the counters.) There's now eleven counters there. How many are hidden under here? (Points to the screen.)

K: (Keeps her hands on the desk for 20 seconds, looking ahead and occasionally glancing at the counters). Ten.

Kelly correctly solved the following four Removed Items tasks: 3 r 1, 5 r 2, 10 r 2, and 27 r 4. On the Removed Items task of 15 r 3, she answered 'eleven' instead of 'twelve'. Her solution to 27 r 4 is described in the following video excerpt.

T: (Places a collection of 27 counters in front of Kelly and places a screen over them.) This time there are twenty-seven, right? (Removes four of the counters and places them under a second screen.) I'm taking four of them out. How many are left under there?

K: (Looks ahead for 22 seconds with her hands on the desk.) Twenty-three.

T: Very good! How did you know there's twenty-three under there? That's right. Did you think?

K: Was twenty-seven. And you take twenty-six and twenty-five and twenty-four and twenty-three away.

Scenario 7: Tanya and Kelly – Solution

Kelly was able to solve additive tasks and Removed Items tasks but was not able to solve Missing Subtrahend tasks. Although Kelly did not count aloud or move her lips, the times taken to solve the tasks are consistent with her using a strategy involving counting-by-ones. Kelly may have been using her fingers under the desk to keep track of her counts. That she could not solve Missing Subtrahend tasks indicates that Kelly was less advanced than Stage 4. Whether Kelly counted-on or counted-from-one when solving the additive tasks is not apparent. Nevertheless her solution of four Removed Items tasks, and her explanation of her solution of '27 r 4' in terms of counting back provides sufficient evidence of advanced counting-by-ones strategies. Therefore Kelly is judged to be at Stage 3, that is, the Initial Number Sequence.

Scenario 8: Joyce and Jed

Jed correctly solved the following five additive tasks: 3 and 2, 5 and 4, 9 and 6, 8 and 5, and 9 and 3. On the first task Jed's solution strategy was not apparent initially. The following video excerpt continues after Jed had answered 'five'.

Jo: How did you count it up?

Je: You just go – one two, three (in co-ordination with three points over a screen covering three counters), four, five (in co-ordination with two points over a screen covering two counters).

Jo: I'm going to take these five disks and put them here (briefly displays and then screens five counters) and I'm going to take four more and put them here (briefly displays and then screens four counters).

Je: (Looks ahead and makes points over the screen covering five counters in co-ordination with subvocal counts.) One, two, three, four, five (makes three points over the second screen in co-ordination with counts), six, seven, eight – (makes four points over the second collection in co-ordination with counts), six, seven, eight, nine!

Following this Jed was presented with the additive task, 9 and 6.

Jo: I'm going to take nine disks and cover them up and I'm going to take six and cover them up (briefly displays and then screens counters as before).

Je: (Slaps his hand on the first screen.) Nine, nine under – nine – nine (makes points over the second screen in co-ordination with counting slowly), ten, ee – leven I think, eleven, twelve, thirteen, fourteen. (Starts counting again from eleven in co-ordination with points over the screen) eleven – eleven, twelve, thirteen, fourteen, fifteen. Fifteen!

Jo: (Points to the first screen.) You thought there were nine under here. (Points to the second screen.) And then you started counting ten, eleven. How did you remember how many were under here (indicates the second screen)?

Je: (Makes two points over the second screen.) Because, I knew there were three right here and three right here, makes six.

The following video excerpt begins after Joyce presented Jed with the next additive task, that is, 8 and 5.

Je: (Points to the screen covering eight counters.) Eight (places his hand above the screen covering five counters and counts aloud in co-ordination with points), nine, (after three seconds) ten, (after eight seconds) eleven, twelve, thirteen, thirteen!

Jo: (Presents the next task, i.e. 9 and 3) I'm going to put nine here and three here.

Je: (Places his hand on the first screen.) Nine – (looks at the second screen and makes three points over the screen in co-ordination with counting), ten, eleven, twelve, twelve!

Jed was presented with two Missing Addend tasks: 4 to 6 and 12 to 15 – and three Missing Subtrahend tasks – 6 to 4, 10 to 6 and 12 to 9. Jed correctly answered only one of these tasks, that is, 6 to 4 and did not appear to have a strategy for either kind of task. For the Missing Addend task of 12 to 15 he answered 'ten'. For the Missing Subtrahend task of 10 to 6 he answered 'one' and then 'two' and for the final Missing Subtrahend task of 12 to 9 he answered 'seven'.

Jed solved three Removed Items tasks, that is, 3 r 1, 5 r 2, 10 r 2, but did not solve the task of 15 r 3, answering 'seventeen'. Jed's solution to the task of 10 r 2 is shown in the following video excerpt.

Jo: (Briefly displays and then screens ten counters.) There are ten there now Jed.

Je: (Raises ten fingers and then puts his hands under the desk.)

Jo: (Removes and screens two counters.) I'm going to take two away. How many did I leave under here?

Je: (Looks at his hands under the desk.)

Jo: (Indicates the top of the desk.) Would you put your hands up here Jed so I can see you work with your hands.

Je: (Places his hands above the desk with five fingers raised on his left hand and three raised on his right hand. Points to each finger on his left hand in co-ordination with counting.) One, two, three, four, five (points to the three raised fingers on his left hand in co-ordination with counting), six, seven, eight, eight!

Scenario 8: Joyce and Jed – Solution
On the basis of his performance on the various subtraction tasks Jed is no more than Stage 3. Although he did solve one Missing Subtrahend task he did not appear to have a general strategy for these tasks,

for example counting-down-to. In similar vein, Jed did not solve the two Missing Addend tasks and apparently did not use counting-up-to to attempt to solve these tasks. Jed also does not appear to have used counting-down-from to solve the Removed Items tasks. What is clear in the descriptions of Jed's solutions is that he used counting-on to solve the three additive tasks of 9 and 6, 8 and 5, and 9 and 3, and counted from one to solve 5 and 4. Why Jed counted-on on the last three tasks is not apparent. His use of counting-on was apparently spontaneous, in that Joyce did not appear to assist him. On the basis of his solutions of the last three additive tasks Jed is judged to be at Stage 3, that is, the Initial Number Sequence. That Jed solved three Removed Items tasks serves to strengthen the case for classifying him at Stage 3.

Scenario 9: Kathryn and James

James was presented with three additive tasks involving two screened collections: 3 and 2, 5 and 4 and 9 and 6. He solved each of these on his first attempt. In solving 3 and 2 he quickly counted subvocally from three to five. In solving 5 and 4 he answered 'nine' quickly and did not appear to count. His solution to 9 and 6 is shown in the following video excerpt.

K: (Poses the task.) Nine and six more?

J: (Looks ahead for ten seconds with hands under the desk.) Fifteen!

K: How did you do that?

J: 'Cos you add 'em up – 'cos umm –, like it – you start from nine and then you count on how much more.

James was presented with four Missing Subtrahend tasks: 3 to 2, 8 to 6, 12 to 9 and 15 to 11. He solved each on his first attempt. His solution to the second, third and fourth tasks are described in the following video excerpt:

K: (Poses the task of 8 to 6.) . . . And I've got six left. How many did I take away?

J: (Looks ahead with his hands under the desk. Answers after three seconds.) Two.

K: How did you know that?

J: 'Cos when that's up to eight, and you say – you take away two you count backwards to two and you got the right answer.

K: (Poses the task of 12 to 9.) . . . Had twelve. Took some away and I've got nine.

J: (As before, looks ahead with his hands under the desk. Answers after six seconds.) Three.

K: That's clever. How did you do that?

J: Well, you start from twelve and you had to count back from twelve to see what number it was.

K: (Poses the task of 15 to 11.) . . . And there's eleven left. How many did I take away?

J: (As before, answers after eight seconds.) Four.

K: Tell me the numbers you said in your head that time.

J: Fifteen, fourteen, thirteen, then twelve.

Following this James solved the following three Removed Items tasks on his first attempt: 3 r 1, 10 r 2, 15 r 3. When solving the first two tasks he responded quickly and on the third he counted subvocally with his hands under the desk and, after ten seconds in all, answered 'twelve'. In explaining his answer he said, '. . . you've got to take away fifteen and fourteen, and then take away thirteen'. James was finally presented with the following three Missing Addend tasks and solved each on his first attempt: 4 to 6, 5 to 9 and 18 to 23. In solving the first task he responded quickly. His methods for solving the second and third were similar to each other in that he looked ahead with his hands under the desk and responded after about six seconds.

Scenario 9: Kathryn and James – Solution

James was able to solve all three types of subtractive tasks as well as additive tasks, and correctly answered all of the tasks presented to him. James' solutions typically involved an advanced counting-by-ones strategy. James used counting-up-from to solve additive tasks, counting-up-to to solve Missing Addend tasks, counting-down-from to solve Removed Items tasks, and counting-down-to to solve Missing Subtrahend tasks. Solving Missing Subtrahend tasks in this way is a strong indication that James was at Stage 4 rather than Stage 3. In solving the additive task of 5 and 4 the indication is that James did not use counting-by-ones because he answered quickly. Also, James may not have used counting-by-ones on the subtractive tasks of 3 r 1, 10 r 2 and 4 to 6, although it is difficult to discern counting-by-ones on tasks such as these where only one or two counts are required. In overall terms, there is little or no evidence to indicate that James is at Stage 5, that is, using a range of non-count-by-ones strategies. Therefore, on the basis of his facile use of advanced counting-by-ones strategies and, in particular, his use of counting-down-to to solve Missing Subtrahend tasks, James is judged to be at Stage 4, the Intermediate Number Sequence.

Scenario 10: Meg and Matthew

Me: Three counters here (momentarily unscreens a collection of three red counters). Two there (momentarily unscreens a collection of two green counters). How many altogether?

Ma: (Quickly raises three fingers on his left hand and then two simultaneously on his right hand. Counts subvocally using his right index finger to point at each raised finger on his left hand and then his left index finger to point at each raised finger on his right hand.) Five!

The next task was similar to the one above and involved five red counters and four green counters. Matthew used an exactly similar strategy and quickly answered 'Nine!' Meg similarly presented the next task involving nine red counters and six green counters.

Me: I have nine counters here and six counters here. How many altogether?

Ma: (Immediately). I don't know. I don't know six and nine because – .

Me: You might be able to work it out a different way.

Despite prompts from Meg, Matthew did not attempt a counting strategy. Meg removed the screens and asked Matthew to count the counters. He quickly counted from one to fifteen pointing at each counter in turn. The next three tasks were presented similarly to those above except that only the first collection was screened. The first task involved five red and two green, the second four and four and the third seven and five. Matthew easily solved the first and second tasks using his fingers as before but was quite unable to solve the third task. Following this Meg asked him to count out thirteen and then eighteen counters from a pile. He solved both tasks by counting quickly from 'one'.

Scenario 10: Meg and Matthew – Solution

Matthew was clearly at least at Stage 1 because he successfully counted collections of 13, 15 and 18 counters. Matthew solved tasks involving two collections in cases where both collections were screened as well as in cases where only one collection was screened. In solving these tasks Matthew always counted from 'one' and thus he was not at Stage 3. Thus we can conclude that Matthew was at Stage 1 or 2. Matthew solved the following four additive tasks, 3 and 2, 5 and 4, 5 and 2, and 4 and 4 using the same strategy for each. This strategy involves raising fingers on his left hand to signify the counters in the first collection, then raising fingers on his right hand to signify the counters in the second collection, and finally counting all of the raised fingers from one. Clearly, this strategy is viable in additive tasks where each addend is not greater than five. On each of the two tasks where one or both addends were greater than five, that is, 9 and 6 and 7 and 5, Matthew did not solve the task and did not appear to have any strategy available to him. Although Matthew may appear to have satisfied the criteria for Stage 2 because he solved four additive tasks in which one or both collections were screened, he is judged to be at Stage 1 rather than Stage 2. His strategy is referred to as 'building perceptual replacements', that is, his raised fingers are the perceptual items that have replaced the screened counters.

Matthew's strategy is a particular case of a strategy commonly used by young children to solve additive and subtractive tasks. In MR we have called this strategy 'counting forward from one three times'. Children typically use this strategy when they have materials which they can form into collections that signify addends, sums, minuends, etc. Thus a child may use counters to solve 9 and 6 by counting out nine counters, then six counters and then counting all of the counters from one to 15. In similar vein, a child may use counters to solve 12 − 9 by counting out 12 counters, then counting out and separating nine of the 12 counters, and then counting the remaining three. When counters are not available a child may use the fingers as in the case of Matthew but, typically, the strategy is viable for addition only when the two addends are no greater than 5, and viable for subtraction only when the minuend is no greater than 10. Children can become quite facile in their use of finger patterns as part of this strategy, for example children will raise fingers simultaneously to signify a number. In solving 5 and 3, for example, a child might raise five fingers on one hand simultaneously, then raise three fingers on the other hand simultaneously, and then answer 'eight' without counting from one.

A comment on teaching can be made at this point. Consider a situation in which children are given the task of working out written additions or subtractions, for example 5 and 2, 3 and 8, 14 − 7, 12 − 10, etc., and are encouraged to use materials to work out their answers. In this situation children typically use the strategy of counting forward from one three times, that is, they count out a number of counters to signify the first number, etc. Doing tasks of this kind is likely to encourage or reinforce the use of strategies involving perceptual counting and thus discourage advancement in terms of SEAL.

The strategy used by Matthew and the corresponding one for

subtraction (as above) should not be confused with advanced count-ing-by-ones strategies in the particular case where the child uses fin-gers to keep track of the number of counts. Thus a child who solves an additive task such as 8 and 5 by raising five fingers in sequence to keep track of counting from 'nine' to 'thirteen' is using a Stage 3 strat-egy and this strategy should not be confused with the strategy of build-ing perceptual replacements. In the case where the child raises five fingers prior to commencing their count this is also classified as a Stage 3 strategy. In similar vein, children at Stage 3 or Stage 4 will use fin-ger patterns to keep track of counting when solving various types of subtractive tasks. As an example, a child at Stage 4 might solve the Missing Subtrahend task of 16 to 12 by raising four fingers in turn while counting from 'fifteen' to 'twelve'. It is conceivable that a child might solve the task of 8 and 5 involving two screened collections by counting from 'one' to 'eight' and then sequentially raising five fin-gers on one hand to keep track of counting from 'nine' to 'thirteen'. This strategy is not very common, probably because children who can use their fingers in this way usually count-on rather than count from one, that is, they are at Stage 3 at least. Nevertheless, the strategy just described would exemplify Stage 2, that is, Figurative Counting.

Scenario 11: Ivan and Rhett

I: I'm going to give you some counters now. (Briefly displays and then screens three red counters.) Three red ones. I'm going to hide them under there. (Briefly displays and then screens two green counters.) And two green ones. Hide them under there. (Waves his hand over both screens.) How many counters have you got altogether?

R: (Counts subvocally while looking straight ahead. Continues in this vein for 30 seconds.) Four.

I: Let's have a look. (Unscreens both collections.)

R: (Beginning with the three red counters, counts subvocally while pointing at each counter in turn. Then looks at Ivan and smiles.) Five.

I: Okay. Let's try this one. This time I'll give you five red ones. (Briefly displays and then screens five red counters.) Now hide those under there. (Places out two green counters which remain unscreened.) And two green ones.

R: (Looks at the two green counters for three seconds and then looks straight ahead for three seconds.) I don't know.

I: (After two seconds.) Can you work it out? Think hard.

R: (Shakes his head indicating 'no'.) (Looks ahead for 23 seconds.) Can't think of it.

I: (Removes the screen.) What about this one as well. What if I give you . . . (pauses).

R: (Beginning with the five red counters, counts subvocally while pointing at each counter in turn.) Seven.

I: Seven right. What if I give you . . . (removes one of the five red counters and screens the remaining four) four red ones . . . (places out two more green counters leaving all four unscreened) and four green ones?

R: (Looks ahead for two seconds and then looks at the four green counters. Counts subvocally while pointing at each counter in turn. Looks up and continues counting subvocally.) Eight?

I: (Removes the screen.)

R: (Beginning with the four red counters, counts subvocally while pointing at each counter in turn. Looks at Ivan and smiles.) Eight.

I: You were right. What about if I give you . . . (places out three more red counters and screens all seven) seven red ones . . . (places out one more green counter and leaves all five unscreened) and five green ones.

R: (Looks ahead for one second and then looks at the five green counters. Counts subvocally while pointing at each counter in turn. Looks up and continues counting subvocally.) Twelve?

I: How did you work that one out?

R: (Looks ahead but does not answer.)

I: (After five seconds.) I saw you doing some things. Can you tell me what you where doing?

R: (Immediately, while smiling.) Counting.

I: What numbers were you counting? (After six seconds.) What did you count?

R: (Looks ahead for five seconds and then points to the unscreened collection of five green counters.) Those, I counted.

I: Yes. (After five seconds, points at the unscreened counters.) There is not twelve there though is there? So how did you know there was twelve?

R: (Shrugs his shoulders.) I don't know.

I: (Unscreens the seven red counters.)

Following this Ivan presented Rhett with three Missing Subtrahend tasks (3 to 2; 8 to 6; 6 to 4) and three Removed Items tasks (3 r 1; 10 r 2; 5 r 2). Rhett solved the introductory tasks only (3 to 2 and

3 r 1) and was generally unsuccessful on the other tasks. On these tasks he did not seem to use a strategy involving counting back, and in most cases his answers seemed to be little more than guesses.

Scenario 11: Ivan and Rhett – Solution

In this scenario Rhett is presented with four additive tasks involving two collections, that is, 3 and 2, 5 and 2, 4, and 4 and 7 and 5. On the first task both collections were screened whereas on the other three tasks, the first mentioned collection only is screened. On the first task Rhett took a relatively long time to answer, that is, 30 seconds, and then answered 'four' rather than 'five'. It is reasonable to assume that because of Rhett's apparent difficulty with this task, Ivan decided that, on subsequent additive tasks, he would unscreen one of the two collections. Although Rhett did not provide any answer on the second task he correctly answered both the third and fourth tasks. It is clear that Rhett counted from one when solving the third and fourth tasks. This and his apparent lack of a strategy to solve subtractive tasks indicates that he was no more than Stage 2.

Rhett's solutions of the third and fourth additive tasks are unusual to some extent. Both tasks involved a screened and an unscreened collection rather than two screened collections, and in both tasks Rhett first counted the unscreened collection rather than the screened collection. In continuing his count, to count the second screened collection, Rhett was able to keep track of four counts in the case of the third task, and seven counts in the case of the fourth task. For this reason Rhett is judged to be at Stage 2, that is, Figurative Counting, rather than Stage 1.

Scenario 12: Sandra and Ben

Ben was presented with five additive tasks involving two collections, that is, 3 and 2, 5 and 4, 9 and 6, 8 and 5, and 9 and 3. On the first task (3 and 2) Ben answered 'five' after eight seconds but his solution strategy was not apparent. His solution to 5 and 4 is shown in the following video excerpt.

S: (Poses the task.) Five and four?
B: (Rubs his face with his right hand.) I know. That . . . that is, ten.
S: (Places a hand on each screen.)
B: (Quickly.) Nine!
S: Pardon?
B: Is it nine?
S: Well you tell me. Five and four?

B: Five and four? Is nine.
S: (Unscreens both collections.) Have a look. See if you were right.
S: (Poses the next task.) Nine and six?
B: (Looks to his right.) Nine and six is sixteen. Actually . . . it is fifteen.
S: How do you know that?
B: (Immediately.) 'Cause, if it was ten it would be sixteen and if it was nine it would be fifteen.
S: (Poses the next task.) What about eight and five? Eight and five?
B: Is ten.
S: (Unscreens both collections).

Ben counted from one to thirteen in co-ordination with pointing at each counter in turn. After a brief discussion Sandra presented the next task.

S: Nine and three?
B: (Immediately.) Nine and three is . . . twelve.
S: How did you get that?
B: (Immediately.) 'Cause, if it was ten and three it would be thirteen and you just cut . . . cut off one.

Sandra then presented Ben with three Missing Addend tasks, that is, 4 to 6, 12 to 15, and 8 to 10. Ben answered 'three' on the first task, and answered the second and third tasks correctly. His strategies for solving these three tasks were not apparent. Following this Ben solved three Missing Subtrahend tasks, that is, 5 to 3, 10 to 6 and 12 to 9. He used a finger pattern for ten to solve the second of these but his strategies for solving the first and third were not apparent. The following video excerpt begins after Ben answered 'three' on the last of these tasks.

S: How did you know that one?
B: 'Cause (raises his thumb), twelve . . . and (raises his point finger) ten . . . (lowers his point finger) twelve, (raises his point finger) and eleven (raises his middle finger), and ten are 'tooken' away and that makes nine.

Following this Ben also solved three Removed Items tasks, that is, 10 r 2, 15 r 3, and 27 r 4. On the last of these he first answered 'twenty-four'. Sandra then indicated that he was incorrect and he answered 'twenty-three'. Ben used his fingers to solve this task, and in doing so, he concealed his fingers. This was the second occasion that he did this, having also concealed his fingers on the Missing Subtrahend task of

10 to 6. In the case of solving 27 r 4 it was likely that Ben used his fingers to keep track of counting back from 27.

Scenario 12: Sandra and Ben – Solution

Ben solved a wide range of additive and subtractive tasks and, although his strategies were often not apparent, it was very clear that he was not counting from one. Thus Ben is at least Stage 3. In explaining the strategy he used to solve the Missing Subtrahend task of 12 to 9, Ben counted-down-to and used his fingers to keep track of three counts. This was indicative of a Stage 4 strategy. In the case of three of the additive tasks Ben indicated that he could use non-count-by-ones strategies. On the first task (5 and 4) he answered 'ten' and then quickly said 'nine'. He did not appear to use a counting strategy on this task and thus it is likely that he used the fact that five and five make ten to work out five and four. In explaining his solution to 9 and 6 he was aware that ten and six make sixteen, and in explaining his solution to 9 and 3 he was aware that ten and three make thirteen. In general terms Ben's solution strategies were not easily discernible. His advanced thinking was more apparent in his explanations than his solutions. Nevertheless he provided three indications of non-count-by-ones strategies and therefore is judged to be at Stage 5, that is, Facile Number Sequence.

Summary

Through careful observation of a child's problem-solving activity during the assessment interview, teachers can determine the child's stage in terms of the SEAL model. This is based on determining the most advanced strategy available to the child.

In Chapter 3 the reader was introduced to MR assessment. The purposes of the assessment tasks were explained and detailed descriptions of some of the important tasks in MR assessment were provided. The next chapter focuses on the preparation and administration of the assessment interview.

6

Preparing for the Assessment Interview

Mathematics Recovery assessment aims to provide extensive and detailed information about the child's numerical knowledge. This includes determining the child's stage and levels in terms of the Learning Framework in Number, and obtaining detailed information about the child's current numerical strategies and knowledge of number words and numerals. This assessment information is crucial in that it enables the teacher to teach at the cutting edge of the child's current knowledge in terms of LFIN. Thus LFIN provides directionality to this teaching. Determining the child's stage in terms of SEAL is a key outcome of the assessment and this involves eliciting during the course of the assessment the child's most advanced numerical strategies.

In order to obtain the required detail of information about the child's numerical knowledge and strategies it is necessary to administer the assessment individually via an interview. The interview is videotaped and the outcomes of the assessment are determined by analysing the videotape of the interview. The process of analysing the assessment interview is discussed in Chapter 7. During the assessment interview the interviewer focuses on determining the child's most advanced numerical strategies in terms of LFIN and obtaining detailed information about the child's numerical knowledge. In doing so, the interviewer takes a somewhat flexible approach which may involve posing additional tasks and questions on the basis of the child's initial responses to the tasks. Because they do not record any information during the course of the interview, the interviewer can focus exclusively on observing and responding to the child on the basis of their ongoing observations and decision-making. As stated in Chapter 3, the assessment consists of two interview schedules, Assessment A and Assessment B. Assessment A is appropriate for all Year 1 children and Assessment B is administered at a later session, to children who are assessed at Stage 3 or higher, on the basis of Assessment A. The assessment interviews are suitable for use with many children in the Kindergarten to Year 3 range.

This chapter focuses on the following four sections:

- Conducting the Assessment Interview.
- Guidelines for Videotaping Assessment Interviews.
- Preparing the Assessment Kit.
- Scripts for Presenting the Assessment Tasks.

Subsequent chapters focus on analysing the assessment interview, using the assessment to plan teaching, and reflecting on teaching.

Conducting the Assessment Interview

In order to properly administer the assessment interview the interviewer needs to learn the words and actions associated with presenting each kind of assessment task, and also to learn the general interview technique, which involves observation and questioning in order to elicit information about the child's knowledge and strategies. This interviewing technique involves the teacher using his or her judgement during the course of the interview to pose additional questions that take account of the child's responses to the assessment tasks.

Becoming competent in administering the assessment requires extensive practice, review and reflection. Learning to conduct the assessment should involve interviews with several children, reviewing videotapes of interviews and then repeating this whole process several times. Much can be learned by closely observing and interpreting videotaped records of children's responses to the assessment tasks. Through practice, review and reflection, the interviewer becomes very attuned to the nature and range of children's responses to the tasks and the techniques involved in posing additional questions when necessary.

Practising the Assessment Interview

Before administering the assessment interview, teachers should practise individually and in pairs, etc. the posing of the various assessment tasks. It is recommended that the first assessments with children be undertaken with more able Year 1 children. These children tend to more readily understand the tasks and are more likely to be successful, and thus it is usually easier to conduct the interview with such children.

Re – posing and Rephrasing Tasks

Administering the interview involves the interviewer following a prescribed schedule and it is important that the tasks are presented as described in the schedule. The interviewer should avoid presenting the task a second time, unless it necessary. This can be particularly counterproductive if the child has already started solving the task, because doing so can interrupt their thought process. In cases where additional clarification for the child seems necessary, the interviewer may re-pose a task and repeat statements in the script. The interviewer may also rephrase or make variations to the verbal instructions, but the nature and conditions of the task should not be varied. In the initial stages of learning to administer the assessment, it is best to follow the scripts closely. With experience the interviewer will become more fluent and flexible in presenting the tasks.

Revisiting Tasks

The interviewer must refrain from providing any verbal or non-verbal clues to the child. The tasks have the purpose of providing insight into the child's numerical thinking, and this information is equally as important as whether the child answers the task correctly. In cases where the interviewer thinks that the child may have made a random error, tasks may be re-posed at a later time during the course of the interview. Thus there is the possibility of revisiting particular tasks if this is considered likely to provide additional information about the child's knowledge and strategies.

Eliciting the Most Advanced Strategy

The importance of closely observing the child's strategy was emphasized above and also in Chapter 3. In order to elicit the child's most advanced strategy it is necessary first to understand the child's current strategy. Eliciting the child's most advanced strategy typically involves asking, 'Can you do that another way?' Alternatively, the interviewer might pose a supplementary task and ask the child if they can work out this problem by a different method.

Monitoring the Child's Ease and Comfort

At the beginning of the interview, the interviewer should take steps to make the child feel as comfortable as possible. As well as asking the child their name and other particulars, the interviewer should explain the purpose of the interview and tell the child what is expected of them during the interview. The interviewer should monitor and be sensitive to the child's state of ease and comfort during the course of the interview.

Use Motivation Sparingly

In most cases it is not necessary to provide ongoing encouragement and motivation to the child because, typically, children seem to gain intrinsic satisfaction from solving the tasks. Thus as a general rule the interviewer should not routinely comment on the correctness of the child's responses. It may be appropriate to do so when, for example, the child expresses particular interest in whether they have answered correctly. Confirming that a child has correctly answered all or most of a group of tasks often seems to have a positive motivational effect on the child. In similar vein, affirming sound effort on the part of the child in attempting to solve tasks usually proves to be motivational when it is genuine and not overdone. Thus it is appropriate to use motivation and encouragement sparingly.

'Talking to the Camera'

This technique involves making a statement during the course of the interview that refers to an observation or realization concerning the child's strategy. The interviewer makes the statement for the purpose of establishing a record on the videotape of their observation or realization. If the interviewer observes that the child used their fingers in a particular way during a solution, for example, the interviewer may comment on this in a non-committal fashion, for example 'I saw you raise four fingers.' This technique should be used in such a way that it causes no disruption to the child and little or no interruption to the flow of the interview.

Introductory Tasks, Entry Tasks, etc.

Most of the Task Groups in Assessment A (all except Forward Number Word Sequence, Subitizing, and Numeral Identification) begin with an introductory task, which familiarizes the child with the new type of task. The introductory task is posed first. If the child has difficulty with the introductory task, the interviewer should explain it thoroughly and work through it with them. If necessary, a second introductory task can be presented. The entry task is now presented. If the child has difficulty with the entry task, the interviewer should present the less advanced tasks. If the child solves the entry task easily, the interviewer should present the more advanced tasks. In some cases it may be appropriate to present the entry task, the less advanced task and the more advanced tasks. Supplementary tasks are presented when additional clarification of a child's strategies is required.

Summary Guidelines for Presenting Assessment Tasks

1. Present the tasks in the order in which they appear in the schedule.
2. Avoid re-posing the task unless you are sure it is necessary.
3. Verbal instructions may be rephrased if it is likely to help the child understand the task.
4. Tasks may be revisited in situations where the child is thought to have made a random error.
5. Give children sufficient time to focus on solving the tasks.
6. Avoid temptations to talk to the child when they are engaged in solving a task.
7. Watch closely for lip, finger, head and body movements that might provide insight into the child's thinking.
8. As a general rule, do not comment on the correctness of the child's response.
9. Be sensitive to the child's state of ease and comfort during the course of the interview and use motivation and encouragement sparingly.
10. Use the technique of 'talking to the camera' if it is likely to be particularly useful to record an observation or realization.

Additive and Subtractive Tasks

In the case of the additive and subtractive tasks, it is particularly important to understand as fully as possible the child's solution strategies. Thus, as a general rule, the interviewer should ask the child how they are solving these tasks, but there are certain provisos to this. Children are sometimes apparently unable to explain their strategy, and children may knowingly or unwittingly describe a strategy that differs from their original strategy. For example, after solving the additive task of 3 + 2 the child might say, 'I counted one, two, three and then four, five', when they actually may have counted-on. Too frequently questioning the child about their solution process can become routine and tedious because the child may tend to respond in a non-reflective way. Thus repeatedly asking the child 'How did you do that?' may be counter-productive. Questions should be as open as possible, for example, avoid dichotomous questions such as 'Did you count? Did you start from seven?', and questions that embody unwarranted assumptions like 'Where did you count from?' Better questioning would be to say, 'I saw you moving your head, what words were you saying?'

Videotaping the assessment interview does not require the presence of an additional person as camera operator.

Judicious questioning of children about their strategies is one of the more challenging requirements of the interview process. Close observation of the child's problem-solving procedures can greatly reduce reliance on their explanations, in order to understand their strategies. Finally, it is often the case that the child's strategy becomes apparent only during the video analysis phase, that is, after the interview has been completed.

Summary Guidelines for Additive and Subtractive Tasks

1. Keep firmly in mind the goal of gaining insight into the child's strategy.
2. Observe the child's solution strategy as closely as possible.
3. When the child has completed their solution, question the child about their strategy. Questions should be tailored as closely as possible to the child's observed strategy.
4. Be careful not to overdo the technique of asking the child how they solved the task.

5. Avoid questions that embody unwarranted assumptions about the child's strategy, and as a general rule, avoid dichotomous questions.
6. Remember that children frequently use strategies that are less sophisticated than those of which they are capable.

Guidelines for Videotaping Assessment Interviews

It is common for teachers initially to be somewhat daunted by the prospect of videotaping their assessment interviews. At the same time the vast majority of teachers quickly gain a level of expertise and the process of videotaping their assessment interviews becomes very routine. No doubt this process is helped by the fact that, after conducting and reviewing a series of interviews, teachers begin to appreciate the power of the videotaping process for learning about children's early numerical knowledge and strategies. Videotaping of the assessment interview does not require the presence of an additional person as camera operator. Thus in the typical situation the interviewer has responsibility for setting up the camera, and switching the record function on and off at the commencement and conclusion respectively of the assessment interview.

Specific guidelines for videotaping assessment interviews are now presented under the following six subheadings: interview room; videotaping equipment; camera and room setup; camera operation; using and labelling videotapes; and conducting the interview.

Interview Room
- If possible, use a room which does not have any light entering from an external source.
- Videotaping is often of better quality if the interviewer wears dark clothing.
- Check beforehand that mains power supply is available and conveniently located. Most cameras have a battery-operation feature that can be used if necessary.
- Minimize noise interference from devices such as air-conditioners or lights by placing the camera and child away from these.
- Turn off heating and air-conditioning fans or vents during the recording process, if possible.

Videotaping Equipment
- If possible, use an external microphone with the videocamera, preferably a uni-directional one.

- Ensure that a sufficient quantity of videotapes is available.
- Rewinding videotapes forward and backward prior to videotaping can help to avoid or reduce tracking problems.
- A quick release tripod is preferable.

Camera and Room Setup

- Mount the camera on a tripod and be sure to remove the lens cap.
- The teacher and child should be seated on the same side of the table and the camera should be placed to face the teacher and child.
- The camera should be pointed away from any outside light source such as windows and glass doors.
- Space should be sufficient to allow both the teacher and the child to be included in the video frame.
- Use a wide-angle setting (i.e. the 'W' button) to locate the camera as closely as possible to the interview table.
- Adjust the zoom lens facility (i.e. W and T buttons) so that the video picture includes the child, the teacher and the tabletop on which the tasks are presented.

Camera Operation

- Set the date and time settings so that these appear on the video-recording. In the case of cameras that do not show date and time displays together, put the time display on and place a sign on the interview table indicating the day's date.
- Ensure that you are familiar with the ON/OFF and STANDBY features of the camera. Some cameras automatically switch to a STANDBY setting during periods when they are not being used.
- Press the RECORD button prior to commencing the interview. The RECORD button is usually a red button and is often located between the W and T buttons on the right hand side of the camera. When the RECORD button is activated a signal, for example 'rec', should appear on the recording screen.
- Some cameras may be supplied with a remote control device that enables you to switch the recording function on and off. Use of such devices is not particularly important in recording the interview.

Using and Labelling Videotapes

- It is helpful to write the school name and date on the outside label, and on the inside label, the date of the interview(s), each child's name, and the commencement time of the interview.

- Immediate labelling of videotapes on completion of filming is recommended.
- The assessment interviews for several children may be recorded on one videotape. Each child should be clearly identifiable via the list of names and times on the inside label.
- Typically, teachers commence the interview session by stating or asking the child's name and other particulars such as class teacher's name, school name and the child's birthdate. This is a useful technique because it helps to ensure accuracy of this kind of information.

Conducting the Interview
- Obtaining high-quality sound recording is very important. The interviewer should attempt to ensure that the child's voice is audible and is recorded as clearly as possible.
- Prior to commencing the assessment interview, complete the required information at the top of the Assessment Schedule. Do not write on the Assessment Schedule when conducting the interview.

Preparing the Assessment Kit

This section provides the information for the reader to assemble the Mathematics Recovery Assessment Kit. The Assessment Kit consists of the interview schedules for Assessment A and Assessment B (included in Chapter 3), and the materials used to present the tasks. These materials can be readily produced and can be aligned with the tasks on the interview schedules. Descriptions of these materials appear below.

Materials for Assessment A
- 67 cards (10cm × 15cm note cards or can be cut from poster board).
- 2 sheets of construction paper (not white) – these will be used for covering counters.
- 27 counters of one colour.
- 6 counters of a second colour.
- 55 black dots (obtained from an office supply – 19mm).

Making the Materials
- *Task Group 5.* Subitizing needs 55 dots, 5 cards with regular patterns (as on dice) and 5 cards with irregular patterns as indicated

in the script for Assessment A.
- *Task Group 6.* Numeral Identification – 23 cards with the appropriate numerals written on them.
- *Task Group 7.* Sequencing numerals – 30 cards (6cm × 6cm) with appropriate numerals written on them. *Note:* Cards must be sufficiently narrow in order to fit in a line across the table.
- *Task Group 8.* Additive Tasks – 2 screens (made from A4 construction paper), 27 counters of one colour and 6 counters of a second colour.
- *Task Group 9.* One card with number phrase written on it (16 – 12).

Materials for Assessment B
- 22 cards – 10cm × 15cm note cards (or cut your own).
- 5 small cards (6cm × 6cm).
- 1 copy of Tens and Ones strips and dots (enlarged as provided in the script for Assessment B).
- 2 sheets of poster board (A4) for covering and uncovering in Task Group 12.
- 1 copy of rows of tens and ones for the uncovering tasks (enlarged) – 2 uncovering tasks.
- 4 sheets of plain copy paper and a marker for writing answers.

Making the Materials
- *Task Group 10.* 15 cards with appropriate tasks written on them. 5 smaller cards with 4, 14, 18, – and = written on them.
- *Task Group 11.* Copy of Tens and Ones cut apart to place on table one at a time. Also, short strips of just four dots and three dots.
- *Task Group 12.* Two covering sheets are required.
- *Task Group 13.* Seven cards with number sentences written on them.

Scripts for Presenting the Assessment Tasks

This section sets out the words and actions used by the interviewer when presenting the assessment tasks. Statements to be made by the interviewer are shown in italics. For each Task Group a concise description is provided setting out the steps taken in presenting the task. Additional guidance for each Task Group is provided in the 'Notes' section which appears after the description.

Assessment A

Task Group 1: Forward Number Word Sequence

Start counting from one and I will tell you when to stop.
When the child reaches 'thirty-two', ask them to stop.
Tasks 1(b), 1(c) and 1(d) are posed similarly.
Notes: The child is not told in advance the number at which they are to stop. As a general rule, children will be able to attempt all four tasks. If the child is proceeding very slowly on a particular task, some or all of the remaining tasks need not be posed.

Task Group 2: Number Word After

I am going to tell you a number and I would like you to tell me what number comes after it. What number comes after one?
Provide clarification if necessary.
What number comes after fourteen?
What number comes after eleven?
Continue with the Entry Task, if the child is not having significant difficulty. Then proceed to the More Advanced Task or Less Advanced Task, as appropriate.

Notes: If the child appears to drop back to 'one' or is unsuccessful on some of the numbers in the Entry Task, proceed to the Less Advanced Task. If the child makes several errors on the Entry Task but is answering with reasonable ease, the More Advanced Task should also be posed, after the Less Advanced Task. If the child confuses number word after and number word before, provide appropriate clarification. Particular items may be revisited.

Task Group 3: Subitizing

I am going to show you some cards that have dots on them and I would like you to tell me how many dots you see.
I am going to show each card very quickly. Ready!
Flash each of the cards in turn, displaying each for half a second.

Notes: Before commencing ensure that the cards are placed into two piles (regular and irregular) and correctly sorted in each pile, that is, as in the schedule. When flashing each card, ensure that you hold it vertically and stationary for the required time, that is, half a second.

Task Group 4: Numeral Identification

I am going to show you some cards which have a number on them.
I would like you to tell me what the number is.

This time I will not be showing the cards quickly so you will have enough time to read the number.
Display the '10' card.
What number is this?
Continue with the Entry Task, displaying each of the cards in turn. Proceed to Less Advanced Task and/or More Advanced Task as appropriate.

Notes: As for Task Group 3, ensure that the cards are placed into three piles and correctly ordered in each pile. If the child does not answer immediately, they may be using a strategy of saying the number word sequence forward. Particular items may be revisited.

Task Group 5 – Backward Number Word Sequence
Would you count from three down to one?
Help the child if necessary.
Would you count from ten down to one?
Would you count down from fifteen and I will tell you when to stop?

Notes: For (b) onward do not tell the child in advance where to stop. If child has significant difficulty on (b) and/or (c), the tasks from (c) or (d) onward may be omitted.

Task Group 6: Number Word Before
I am going to tell you a number and I would like you to tell me what number comes before it. What number comes before two?
Provide clarification if necessary.
What number comes before twenty-four?
What number comes before seventeen?
Continue with the Entry Task, if the child is not having significant difficulty. Then proceed to the More Advanced Task or Less Advanced Task, as appropriate.

Notes: If the child appears to drop back to 'one' or is unsuccessful on some of the numbers in the Entry Task, proceed to the Less Advanced Task. If the child makes several errors on the Entry Task but is answering with reasonable ease, the More Advanced Task should also be posed, after the Less Advanced Task. If the child confuses number word before and number word after, provide appropriate clarification. Particular items may be revisited.

Task Group 7: Sequencing Numerals
Arrange the ten cards randomly on the table in front of the child.

I would like you to arrange these cards in order from smallest to largest.
Indicate a convenient position on the child's left-hand side.
Start by putting the smallest down here.
Similarly present the Less Advanced Task and/or More Advanced Task as appropriate.

Notes: Cards should be placed into three piles and randomly ordered in each pile.
The child reads the card for the camera.

Task Group 8: Additive Tasks
Introductory Task:
Briefly display and then screen three counters. *Here are three red counters.*
Briefly display and then screen two counters. *Here are two green counters. How many counters are there altogether?*
If necessary explain the task to the child.
Similarly pose the two Entry Tasks.
If necessary pose the Less Advanced Tasks involving partial screening and/or the tasks involving visible collections of 13 and 18 counters (see below).

Entry Task:
As per Introductory Task.

Partially Screened Task:
Briefly display and then screen five counters. *Here are five red counters.*
Display two green counters. *Here are two green counters. How many counters are there altogether?*

Counting Collections:
Place out a collection of 13 red counters. *Would you please count to see how many counters there are altogether in this group?*
Similarly pose the task involving 18 counters.

Missing Addend Task:
Briefly display and then screen four red counters. *Here are four red counters.*
Place two green counters under a screen without allowing the child to see them. *With these counters altogether there are six counters. How many counters are there under this screen?*

Notes: Use counters of two different colours, one colour for each addend. Do not count out the counters when placing out each collection. The Supplementary Tasks are posed if more information is required about the child's strategy. Similarly, Missing Addend Tasks are presented if necessary. Observe the child closely, including their fingers, in order to try to determine their strategy. If appropriate, ask the child to explain their strategy.

Refer also to the descriptions of these tasks that appear in Chapter 3.

Task Group 9: Subtractive Tasks
Written Task:
Place the card in front of the child (16 − 12). *Would you please read this card?*
Do you have a way of working that out?
(If necessary, repeat with 14 − 10.)

Missing Subtrahend Tasks:
Briefly display and then screen five counters. *Here are five counters.*
Ask the child to look away while you remove and screen two of the counters (using a second screen). *I had five counters, then I took some of those away and now I have three only. How many counters did I take away?*
Similarly pose the two Entry Tasks (10 to 6 and 12 to 9).
If the child has difficulty with the Entry Tasks, present the Less Advanced Task.
Pose the Supplementary Task if more information is required about the child's strategy.

Removed Items Tasks:
Briefly display and then screen three counters. *Here are three counters.*
Ask the child to look away while you remove and screen one of the counters (using a second screen). *I had three counters, then I took one away. How many counters are there left under this screen?*
Similarly pose the two Entry Tasks (10 r 2 and 15 r 3).
Use the Less Advanced Task and Supplementary Task as appropriate.

Notes: Observe the child closely, including their fingers, in order to try to determine their strategy. If appropriate, ask the child to explain their strategy.

Refer also to the descriptions of these tasks that appear in Chapter 3.

Assessment B

Task Group 10: Tasks to Elicit Non-Count-By-Ones Strategies

Task (a):

Place out the blank sheet for writing and place the '9 + 3' card on top of the blank sheet. *Can you work this out?*

Write '= 12' to the right of '9 + 3'. Place the '9 + 4' card below the '9 + 3' card. Indicate the cards in turn. *Can you use this to help you work out this?*

What is the answer?

Indicating appropriately. *How did you use this to work out this?*

Similarly 9 + 5, 9 + 6.

Task (b):

Ask the child to work out 6 + 6, and write the answer to the right. Place the '7 + 5' card below the '6 + 6' card. Indicate the cards in turn. *Can you use this to help you work out this?*

What is the answer?

Indicating appropriately. *How did you use this to work out this?*

Similarly, 8 + 4.

Task (c):

Ask the child to work out 7 – 5, and write the answer to the right. Place the '27 – 5' card below the '7 – 5' card. Indicate the cards in turn. *Can you use this to help you work out this?*

What is the answer?

Indicating appropriately. *How did you use this to work out this?*

Similarly, 47 – 5.

Task (d):

Ask the child to work out 15 + 3, and write the answer to the right. Place the '18 – 3' card below the '15 + 3' card. Indicate the cards in turn. *Can you use this to help you work out this?*

What is the answer?

Indicating appropriately. *How did you use this to work out this?*

Task (e):

Place out the '21 – 16 = 5' card. Place the '21 – 5' card below the '21 – 16 = 5' card. *If I tell you that 21 take away 16 is 5, can you use this to help you work out this?*

Indicating appropriately. *How did you use this to work out this?*

Task (f):

Place out the '14 + 4 = 18' card. *Can you read this sentence for me?* Place out the cards for '14', '4', '18', '=', and ' – '. *Can you use these three numbers and these two cards to make a take away?* If successful ask *Do you have another way of making a subtraction sentence?*

Task Group 11: Tens and Ones Tasks
Counting by Tens with Strips Task:
Place out one Ten Strip. *How many are there?*
If the child answers 'one' ask how many dots there are.
Allow the child to count the dots if they wish.
Place out a second Ten Strip. How many are there now?
Continue placing out an additional Ten Strip up to eight in all, each time asking the child how many.
Pick up all eight Ten Strips. *How many dots were there? How many strips were there?*

Incrementing by Tens:
Place out the Four Strip. *How many dots are there?*
Place a Ten Strip to the right of the Four Strip. *How many dots are there now?*
Continue placing out Ten Strips and, on each occasion, asking how many dots in all.
If necessary, repeat the task starting with a Three Strip or a Seven Strip.

Notes: On the first task, try to ensure that the child understands that there are ten dots on each Ten Strip. Observe closely to ascertain whether or not the child is incrementing by tens, counting-on by ones, or perhaps counting from one on each occasion.

Task Group 12: Uncovering Tasks
Task (a):
Cover all of the dots. Move the screen to the right in order to uncover the first Ten Strip. *How many dots are there?* Continue as indicated, and on each occasion ask the child how many dots there are altogether:
One strip (10); three dots (13); two strips (33); four dots (37); three dots (40); now use a second screen to cover the 40 dots and then uncover the next strip (50); two dots (52); two strips (72).

Task (b):
As before, uncover the dots and strips as indicated and on each occasion ask the child how many dots there are altogether:
Four dots (4); one strip (14); two strips (34); now use a second screen

to cover the 34 dots and then uncover one strip and two dots (46); two strips and five dots (71).

Task Group 13: Horizontal Sentences

Place out the '16 + 10' card and ask the child if they know the answer.
Place out the '16 + 9' card.
Indicating appropriately. *Can you use this to work out this?*
Place out the '42 + 23 =' card. *Can you work this out?*
Similarly, 38 + 24.
Present 39 + 53 if you are unsure of the child's strategy.
Similarly present 56 − 23, and 43 − 15.

Notes: On each task, observe closely to try to ascertain the child's strategy.

Summary

Assessment in MR involves an individually administered assessment interview which is videotaped for subsequent analysis. The assessment consists of two parts: Assessment A can be administered to all first-graders and is suitable for many children in the K–3 ranges. Assessment B is administered to children who attain at least Stage 3 on Assessment A. Preparing for the assessment interviews includes organizing a suitable room in which to conduct interviews, obtaining a suitable video camera and learning to operate it, and preparing the assessment kit.

Learning to administer the assessment interview involves teachers in learning the words and actions associated with presenting each kind of assessment task, and also learning the general interview technique of observation and questioning in order to elicit information about the child's knowledge and strategies. Becoming adept at the assessment procedure requires practice, review and reflection. Teachers should practise presenting the assessment tasks with colleagues, and conduct and review a series of assessment interviews with children. Teachers who learn to assess children in this way will gain significant insight into children's early numerical knowledge and strategies.

7

Coding and Analysing the Assessment Interview

This chapter focuses on analysis of the assessment interviews via a system of coding the child's responses to the assessment tasks. The Learning Framework in Number is used to determine the child's stage and levels that are recorded on the Assessment Schedule for each child. The completed assessment schedule is used to develop an individual teaching plan for the child.

Analysis of the Mathematics Recovery (MR) assessment involves viewing the videotape of the assessment in conjunction with annotating the Assessment Schedule. The analyser works from the Assessment Schedule, and each Task Group is analysed in turn, using the Coding System. In this way the completed Assessment Schedule constitutes a written summary of the assessment interview. The final phase of analysis involves determining the child's Stage and Levels in terms of the models in Strands A and B of the Learning Framework in Number.

Coding the Assessment Schedule

A coding system is used to derive the maximum information from a child's performance in the assessment interview. It is assumed that the interview was videotaped and therefore the coding system can be applied as the tape is viewed. The codes indicate how the child responded as well as the answers given. The codes can also indicate how the interview was conducted. The codes are illustrated in Table 7.1.

The code sheet is self-explanatory but it may be useful to exemplify certain aspects. For example, the interviewer wants to know not only the answer the child gives but also the confidence level displayed.

Correct answers are ticked but two ticks can be given indicating a swift, confident response. Errors may be marked with a cross but it is advisable to write down the actual response the child offers. In this way the interviewer can see the incorrect response but we may also be able to detect a pattern of incorrect responses. For example, it is

Table 7.1   The Mathematics Recovery coding schedule

✓	correct
✓✓	correct and with confidence
??	needs time to think
?✓	needs some time, then correct
?✗	needs some time, then incorrect
✗	incorrect (but note error)
✗✓	initially incorrect, then correct
—	child says nothing
SC	child self-corrects
⋀	omission of a number in FNWS or BNWS
IDK	child says 'I don't know'
" "	indicates the words used
Rev	assessor revisits an item
C.from 1	child counts from one
CO	child counts on
CDF	child counts down from
CDT	child counts down to

common in the Numeral Identification tasks for children to reverse responses, saying 'fifty-one' for 15 and 'thirty-one' for 13. It is also desirable to record omissions, or repetitions, in the utterance of number sequences.

It is interesting to note how much thinking time the child required before producing an answer. A question mark or multiple question marks can be used for thinking time. Sometimes a child answers incorrectly and checks themself before giving a correct response. Where the child has corrected an answer without any prompting from the interviewer we use the code 'SC'. Often children say 'I don't know' and, having decided whether to accept this, 'IDK' is recorded.

We want to give the children every opportunity to respond and questions can be restated and rephrased. A useful strategy is to note errors and where there is evidence that this may be an oversight or slip the question can be revisited at the end of a sequence. The code used is 'Rev'.

It is advisable, particularly in the additive and subtractive tasks in Assessment A, and later in the non-count-by-one task items in Assessment B, to record the actual explanations the child offers. Indications of finger movements and specific non-verbal gestures often reveal the strategies a child is using and these should be noted. If a strategy is detected then it is helpful to record this to serve as a reminder when analysing and determining the final Stage of Early Arithmetical Learning and levels. For example, you may code the

child's 'count-on' (CO) or 'count-down-from' (CDF) strategy.
  Comprehensive application of coding will allow:

- the strengths and weaknesses of a child to be detected;
- the identification of patterns of response;
- the correct identification and allocation of levels and stages; and
- an accurate, concise description of the child's ability.

The application of coding will also allow the interviewer to reflect on his or her own performance in administering the task items. For example, one might check whether certain items could have been re-posed or revisited. The ability to rewind the tape and watch the same episode again allows accurate judgements to be made.

Determining the Child's Stage and Levels

Determining the child's stage or level on each of the five models is an important outcome of the assessment. The stage and levels constitute a succinct summary of the extent of the child's early number knowledge. In determining each stage or level, the analyser uses the information from particular Task Groups from the Assessment Schedule. Table 7.2 indicates, for each model, which Task Groups contribute to the determination of the stages or levels of the model.

Determining the Child's Stage

As shown in Table 7.2, Task Groups 8, 9 and 10 are used to determine the child's stage in terms of the SEAL model. Chapters 4 and 5 contain many examples of children's solutions to tasks from Task Groups 8 and 9 (i.e. Assessment A). These examples illustrate strategies that are characteristic of each of the stages in the SEAL model. Thus the examples in Chapters 5 and 6 are most relevant to the issue of determining the child's stage. Table 7.3 lists the Task Groups which are significant at each of Stage 0–5 on the SEAL model.

As indicated in Table 7.3, the child's performance on Task Group 8 is significant at all stages of SEAL. Therefore, in determining the child's stage the analyser should first consider the child's performance on the Entry Tasks in Task Group 8, that is additive tasks such as 5 and 4 and 9 and 6, and also the supplementary additive tasks (8 and 5, 9 and 3) if these were used. The child who exhibits a viable strategy for these tasks is likely to be at Stage 2 at least. The child who seems not to have a strategy to solve these tasks is likely to be Stage 0 or 1 (see Table 7.3).

Table 7.2   Tasks Group(s) considered for a given model

Task Group	Assess. Int.	Model				
		SEAL	FNWS	BNWS	Numeral Ident'n	Tens and Ones
1	A		X			
2	A		X			
3	A					
4	A				X	
5	A			X		
6	A			X		
7	A					
8	A	X				
9	A	X				
10	B	X				
11	B					X
12	B					X
13	B					X

Judging on the Basis of the Most Advanced Strategy

When determining the child's stage it is important to remember that the child is judged on the basis of the most advanced strategy they use. In all of the additive and subtractive tasks, the interviewer should attempt to elicit the most advanced strategies. In the discussions in the following paragraphs the term 'at least' is often used as a qualifier, for example 'the child who correctly counts these [visible] collections is judged to be at Stage 1 at least' and 'the child who counts-down-to to solve Missing Subtrahend tasks is judged to be at Stage 4 at least'. A child might count-down-to on Missing Subtrahend tasks and use Stage 5 strategies on other tasks. In this case the child is judged to be Stage 5. In similar vein, the child who counts from one to solve additive tasks, counts-on to solve Missing Addend and counts-down-from to solve Removed Items is judged to be at Stage 3 (assuming they do not use Stage 4 or Stage 5 strategies).

Table 7.3   Significant tasks for a given Stage of Early Arithmetical Learning

	Stage	Significant tasks
Stage 0:	Emergent Counting	8
Stage 1:	Perceptual Counting	8
Stage 2:	Figurative Counting	8
Stage 3:	Initial Number Sequence	8, 9
Stage 4:	Intermediate Number Sequence	8, 9
Stage 5:	Facile Number Sequence	8, 9, 10

Stage 0 or Stage 1?
The need to distinguish between Stage 0 and Stage 1 is likely to arise in cases where the interviewer has presented the two items in Task Group 8(b) that involve counting unscreened collections of 13 and 18 counters. The child who is unable to count these collections because they omit some of the counters, or do not correctly co-ordinate the number words with the counters, or because they apparently do not know the FNWS, is judged to be at Stage 0. The child who correctly counts these collections is judged to be at Stage 1 at least. In most cases, because the interviewer decided to present these tasks on the basis of their performance on the Entry Tasks, the child is no more advanced than Stage 1.

Stage 1 or Stage 2?
The need to distinguish between Stage 1 or Stage 2 arises when the child uses particular finger patterns to solve the additive tasks of 3 and 2 (i.e. the introductory example) and 5 and 4, and unsuccessfully attempts to use finger patterns to solve tasks such as 9 and 6, 8 and 5, etc. Matthew in Chapter 5, exemplifies this case. His raised fingers constitute perceptual replacements for the screened counters and he establishes his finger patterns prior to commencing to count both collections. In this case the child is classified at Stage 1 only. Distinguishing between Stage 1 and Stage 2 also arises in cases where the child solves tasks involving one screened collection and one unscreened collection. If the child counts the unscreened collection first, and then keeps track while continuing in order to count the screened collection, the child is judged to be at Stage 2, with the proviso that the child's use of this strategy is not limited to the additive task of 5 and 2. Thus it is necessary that the child use this strategy on one or both of the tasks of 4 and 4 and 7 and 5. In the case where the child counts the screened collection first and then continues in order to count the unscreened collection, the child is judged to be at Stage 1. In this case the means by which the child has counted the screened collection does not constitute figurative counting.

Stage 2 or Stage 3?
Distinguishing between Stage 2 and Stage 3 is usually unproblematic. In the case where the child counts-on to solve additive tasks but does not seem to understand the Missing Addend tasks, the child is judged to be at Stage 3 at least. Thus it is sufficient to use counting-on to solve additive tasks only. In many cases children who do not seem to

understand Missing Addend tasks will count-down-from on the Removed Items tasks as well as count-on for additive tasks.

Stage 3 or Stage 4?
The child who counts-down-to to solve Missing Subtrahend tasks is judged to be at Stage 4 at least. Counting-down-to to solve the written task of 16 − 12 (Task Group 9) is also indicative of Stage 4. Attempting to solve Missing Subtrahend tasks or the written task of 16 − 12 by counting-down-from is not indicative of Stage 4, for example the child attempts to count down 12 counts from 16. Children may count-up-to to solve Missing Subtrahend tasks although this is not a common occurrence. One might say these children interpret a Missing Subtrahend task as they might interpret a Missing Addend task. In such cases the child is judged to be at least at Stage 4. Their ability to conceptualize the task in this way is regarded as indicative of Stage 4 rather than Stage 3.

The Stage 5 Child
Stage 5 is characterized by the use of non-count-by-ones strategies, that is strategies which include procedures which do not involve counting by ones. There are many instances where a child uses several Stage 5 strategies in the course of solving tasks in Task Groups 8 and 9 (i.e. Assessment A). As a general rule, at least three instances of Stage 5 strategies on Assessment A are necessary for the child to be judged to be at Stage 5. In the case of children who show one or two instances only, solutions in Task Group 10 (Assessment B) should also be considered. Experience has shown that in Task Group 10, for many children, their response is indicative of Stage 5 on some but not all of the six items. The criterion stated above is applied in the same way: the child is judged to be at Stage 5 if they show at least three instances of Stage 5 strategies across Tasks Groups 8, 9 and 10. In this way the criterion can be applied to Assessment A only, Assessment B only, or collectively across both assessments.

Determining the Child's Levels

This section focuses on determining the child's level on the four models of FNWS, BNWS, Numeral Identification, and Tens and Ones. In some cases within each of the four models, particular tasks are significant for particular levels only, for example, in the case of the FNWS model, Task 2(c), which involves saying the number word after a given number word in the range 'thirty' to 'one hundred', is not significant for Levels 0, 1, 2 or 3, which are concerned with number word facility in the range 'one' to 'ten' only. Tables 7.4–7.7 show, for each of the models in turn, the tasks that are significant for each level in the model.

Determining the Child's FNWS Level

As shown in Table 7.2, Task Groups 1 and 2 are used to determine the child's FNWS level. Table 7.4 lists the tasks which are significant at each of Levels 0–5 on the FNWS model. A child is assessed at Level 2, for example, if, in Task 1(a) the child produces the FNWS to 'ten'

Table 7.4   Significant tasks for a given FNWS level

	Level	*Significant tasks*
Level 0:	Emergent FNWS	1(a)
Level 1:	Initial FNWS up to 'ten'	1(a), 2(b)
Level 2:	Intermediate FNWS up to 'ten'	1(a), 2(b)
Level 3:	Facile with FNWSs up to 'ten'	1(a), 2(b)
Level 4:	Facile with FNWSs up to 'thirty'	1(a), 2(a), 2(b)
Level 5:	Facile with FNWSs up to 'one hundred'	1(a), 1(b), 1(c), 1(d), 2(a), 2(b), 2(c)

Table 7.5   Significant tasks for a given BNWS level

	Level	*Significant tasks*
Level 0:	Emergent BNWS	5(a)
Level 1:	Initial BNWS up to 'ten'	5(a), 6(b)
Level 2:	Intermediate BNWS up to 'ten'	5(a), 6(b)
Level 3:	Facile with BNWSs up to 'ten'	5(a), 6(b)
Level 4:	Facile with BNWSs up to 'thirty'	5(a), 5(b), 5(c), 5(d), 6(a), 6(b)
Level 5:	Facile with BNWSs up to 'one hundred'	5(a), 5(b), 5(c), 5(d), 5(e), 5(f), 6(a), 6(b), 6(c)

Table 7.6   Significant tasks for a given Numeral Identification level

	Level	*Significant tasks*
Level 0:	Emergent Numeral Identification	4(b)
Level 1:	Numerals to '10'	4(b)
Level 2:	Numerals to '20'	4(a), 4(b)
Level 3:	Numerals to '100'	4(a), 4(b),
Level 4:	Numerals to '1000'	4(a), 4(b), 4(c)

Table 7.7   Significant tasks for a given Tens and Ones level

	Level	Significant tasks
Level 1:	Initial Concept of Ten	11, 12
Level 2:	Intermediate Concept of Ten	11, 12
Level 3:	Facile Concept of Ten	11, 12, 13

at least, and answers each of the items in Task 2(a) correctly but uses the strategy of dropping back on some or all of the items in Task 2(a). Experience has shown that children's facility in terms of Task Group 1 may extend over a greater range of numbers than their facility in terms of Task Group 2. Thus children judged to be at Level 1, because they are unable to produce the number word after each of the number words in the range 'one' to 'ten', may well be able to produce the FNWS from 'one' to well beyond 'ten'. In similar vein, children judged to be at Level 4, because they are unable to, in every case, produce the number word after a given number word in the range 'one' to 'one hundred', may be successful on all of the tasks in Task Group 1.

Determining the Child's BNWS Level
As shown in Table 7.2, Task Groups 5 and 6 are used to determine the child's BNWS level. Table 7.5 lists the tasks which are significant at each of Levels 0–5 on the BNWS model. A child is assessed at Level 4, for example, if they answer correctly Tasks 5(a), 5(b), 5(c), that part of 5(d) involving numbers in the range 1 to 30, and each of the items in 6(a) and 6(b) without using the strategy of dropping back; and do not answer correctly one of the following – 5(e), 5(f), that part of 5(d) involving numbers beyond 30, or one or more of the items in Task 6(c).

Determining the Child's Numeral Identification Level
As shown in Table 7.2, Task Group 4 is used to determine the child's Numeral Identification level. Table 7.6 lists the tasks which are significant at each of Levels 0–4 on the Numeral Identification model. A child is assessed at Level 2, for example, if they answer correctly Task 4(a) and items in Task 4(b) involving numerals up to 20, but not some of the items in Task 4(b) involving numerals beyond 20.

Determining the Child's Tens and Ones Level
As shown in Table 7.2, Task Groups 11, 12 and 13 are used to determine the child's Tens and Ones level. Table 7.7 lists the tasks which

are significant at each of Levels 1–3 on the Tens and Ones model. Of significance is whether, on the parts of these tasks where there is an increment by one ten or several tens, the child counts from one, counts-on by ones, or counts by tens. Note that on some parts of the uncovering tasks (Task Group 12) the child has little choice but to count by ones. In cases involving an increment by one ten or several tens, a child might be observed to use more than one of these strategies and in such cases it is the child's most advanced strategy that is significant. Thus a child might count-on by ones on a part of Task 11(b) and from then onward, count by tens. In such cases the child is assessed to be at Level 2 at least. In the case of Level 3, Task 13 is particularly significant. Of interest is whether the child counts by tens or counts by ones only, on these tasks. Note that it is not necessary for the child to answer all of these tasks correctly. Rather, it is sufficient to show clear examples of counting by tens. Strategies that involve adding or subtracting tens are also sufficient for Level 3.

Examples of Children's Non-Standard Responses

The term 'non-standard responses' is used to include incorrect responses, for example confusing number word after and number word before, and immature responses, for example dropping back to one on a number word after task. In the task groups involving number word sequences and numeral identification there are many examples of non-standard responses that are relatively common among young children. This section presents examples of these, that is, children's non-standard responses for Task Groups 1, 2, 4, 5 and 6. These Task Groups are associated with the three models of FNWS (Task Groups 1 and 2), Numeral Identification (Task Group 4) and BNWS (Task Groups 5 and 6).

Task Group 1: Forward Number Word Sequence
Examples of children's non-standard responses on Task Group 1:

1. Non-number words are included in an FNWS, for example 'one, two, three, dog, cat, elephant'.
2. An idiosyncratic FNWS is used, for example ' . . . eleven, twelve, sixteen, nine, four'.
3. One or more of the number words in an FNWS are omitted, for example ' . . . ten, eleven, fourteen, fifteen . . .'.
4. Teen number words in an FNWS are confused with decade number words, for example ' . . . twelve, thirty, forty . . .'.

5. Twenty-ten is said after twenty-nine, that is, ' . . . twenty-eight, twenty-nine, twenty-ten . . .'.
6. Decade number words are omitted from an FNWS, for example ' . . . fifty-eight, fifty-nine, sixty-one . . .'.
7. The incorrect decade number is used, for example ' . . . seventy-eight, seventy-nine, forty, forty-one . . .'.
8. Two hundred is said after one hundred and nine, that is, ' . . . one hundred and eight, one hundred and nine, two hundred, two hundred and one . . .'.

Task Group 2: Number Word After
Examples of children's non-standard responses on Task Group 2:

1. Drops back to one to work out the number word after, that is, after seven – 'one, two . . . seven, eight, eight!'
2. Confuses number word after and number word before, for example four after five.
3. In the case of a decade number, says the next decade number, for example eighty after seventy.
4. In the case of a 'nine' number, says the incorrect decade number, for example seventy after fifty-nine.
5. Says a decade number instead of a teen number, for example fifty after fourteen.

Task Group 4: Numeral Identification
Examples of children's non-standard responses on Task Group 4:

1. Identifies a two-digit numeral beyond 20 as if its digits where in the reverse order, for example '47' is identified as 'seventy-four'.
2. Difficulty in identifying '12'.
3. Identifies '12' as 'twenty-one'.
4. Says the forward number word sequence to identify a numeral, for example to identify '8', 'one, two . . . eight!'
5. Uses decade names for teen numbers, for example '15' is identified as 'fifty'.

Task Group 5: Backward Number Word Sequence
Examples of children's non-standard responses on Task Group 5:

1. One or more of the number words in a BNWS are omitted, for example 'fifteen, fourteen, twelve, eleven . . .'.
2. Decade number words in a BNWS are omitted, for example ' . . . thirty-four, thirty-three, thirty-two, thirty-one, twenty-nine, . . .'.

3. Goes back eleven when reaching the decade, for example 'seventy-two, seventy-one, sixty, sixty-nine, sixty-eight, sixty-seven'.

Task Group 6: Number Word Before
Examples of children's non-standard responses on Task Group 6:

1. Drops back to one to work out the number word before, for example before 'seven', 'one, two, . . . six, seven, six!'
2. Confuses number word before and number word after, for example nine before eight.
3. In the case of a decade number, says the next decade number, for example twenty before thirty.
4. Says a decade number instead of a teen number, for example sixty before seventeen.

8

Learning from Mathematics Recovery

Working with teachers on the development of Mathematics Recovery involved taking a problem-based approach to teachers' learning. In this approach important issues concerning the programme arose almost on a daily basis. The problem-based approach involved discussing issues in weekly teachers' meetings, suggesting appropriate courses of action and seeking feedback through observation and further discussion. Discussion of issues included reviewing current practice and research. Participating teachers also undertook action research projects that aimed to illuminate key issues. This chapter provides an overview of many of these issues under the headings of issues in assessment, issues in teaching, and programmatic issues.

Issues in Assessment

Outcomes of MR Assessment

Mathematics Recovery assessment has the purpose of comprehensively documenting the child's current strategies and knowledge in early number. Determining the child's current stage and levels is one main outcome of assessment but it is important to keep in mind that the assessment is designed to provide much more than the stage and levels. The outcomes of the assessment can be organized into three categories:

1. the child's stage and levels which are recorded at the top of the Assessment Schedule after analysis;
2. the completed Assessment Schedule;
3. the videotape of the interview.

These categories can be thought of as three levels of information:

- the stage and levels provide a brief summary of the child's current knowledge;
- the completed Assessment Schedule provides detailed written information about the child's response on each task;

- the videotape provides a rich and less structured array of information about the child's knowledge and strategies.

The term 'strategies' includes not only those used in tasks associated with the stages of early numerical learning but also strategies used in other tasks, for example numeral identification strategies, numeral sequencing strategies and strategies for determining a number word before.

Variability among MR Participants

In the various implementations of MR there has always been a good deal of variability in early number knowledge among the participating children. This variation is often quite marked among the participants within a given class or school. Additionally, for a given child there is a high degree of commensurability among the four aspects of the assessments. Table 8.1 shows three exemplary assessment profiles of children prior to participating in the programme. These profiles are very typical among participants and collectively they illustrate both the variability among children and, for a given child, the commensurability

Table 8.1 Exemplary assessment profiles of MR participants

Type	Stage	FNWS	BNWS	N. Id.	Summary description
A	0	1	0	0	Cannot count perceptual items, can say the number words from 1 to 10 but has no other facility with number words forward or backward, and cannot identify some or all numerals in the range 1 to 10.
B	1	3	1	1	Counts perceptual items but typically cannot solve tasks when one or both collections are covered, facile with number words forward in the range 1 to 10, can say the words from 10 back to 1 but has no other facility with BNWS, and can identify numerals to 10 but none or few beyond 10.
C	2	4	3	1	Solves some additive tasks involving screened collections and counts from one when doing so, facile with number words forward in the range 1 to 30 and number words backward in the range 1 to 10, and can identify numerals to 10 and many but not all in the range 11 to 20.

across the four aspects of the assessment. Type A profile, for example, shows that a child who is at Stage 0 and at Level 1 on FNWS is likely to be at very low levels on BNWS and Numeral Identification.

Purpose of Videotaping

Use of videotaping in school-based assessment is not common, although in recent years videotaping for various purposes has become more frequent in schools. In MR videotaping of assessment interviews has a central role and videotaping accompanied by retrospective analysis results in a distinctive approach to assessment. Assessment methods in which the teacher's role is to make written records, during the course of the interview, that document the child's responses, require the teacher to direct a great deal of their attention to the details of the recording process. In contrast, in MR assessment the teacher can focus all of their attention on the processes of eliciting the child's strategies and finding the extent of the child's current knowledge. Clearly, the teacher's frame of mind and view of their purpose is quite different in MR assessment from that in assessment involving on-going recording. Thus teachers with training and experience in assessment using ongoing recording usually find that some adjustment is necessary in order to learn this assessment procedure.

Revisiting Assessment Tasks

The question of whether it is appropriate to revisit tasks, that is, to present tasks on a second occasion during the assessment interview, is frequently discussed at teachers' meetings. No doubt the question arises because in approaches to assessment involving comparisons among children, there typically is a requirement that each item is presented to each child in precisely the same way, and that this is necessary to ensure that the assessment is valid. Given that the purpose in MR assessment is to elicit the child's knowledge and most advanced strategies, then it is legitimate to vary task presentation and to revisit tasks when there is a good reason to do so. Thus presenting tasks on a second occasion is regarded as appropriate in particular cases. Revisiting the task for the purpose of eliciting the most advanced strategy should be clearly distinguished from suggesting a strategy to the child or modelling a strategy, for example counting-on. Assessment has the purpose of documenting spontaneous strategies rather than those initiated by the teacher.

In the case of a number word or Numeral Identification task, for example, if the child makes one or two mistakes only, there may be reason to believe that these are careless errors. Following is a technique that can be used to revisit tasks involving number words or Numeral Identification. Suppose, for example, that a child incorrectly identifies '13' as '30', but is successful on the other Numeral Identification tasks in the range 1 to 20. The interviewer does not re-pose the task immediately and does not give any indication that the child is incorrect. The interviewer makes a mental note to revisit the task, that is, to re-pose the task later in the interview and does so after completing a subsequent Task Group of the schedule.

Taking a Flexible Approach to Assessment

When a teacher first learns to administer the assessment schedule there are very good reasons for closely following the schedule and the accompanying script. It is necessary and important to do this in order to learn how to present tasks correctly, for example the various kinds of addition and subtraction tasks. As one becomes skilled and experienced in administering the assessment one learns to take a somewhat flexible approach. For example, the interviewer may pose additional tasks, that is, different from the supplementary tasks on the schedule, when one believes this may help to understand the child's strategy or elicit a more powerful strategy. The interviewer also becomes much more skilful at knowing when continuing with more advanced tasks is unlikely to be fruitful. With experience, interviewers can find the appropriate balance between the need for MR assessment to be standardized to some extent to allow comparisons among children and comparisons of a child's responses at different times, and the need for the assessment to be flexible to allow the interviewer to document efficiently and comprehensively the child's knowledge and strategies.

Reasons for Not Recording During the Interview

As explained in Chapter 6, during the course of the interview, the interviewer should not attempt to record the child's results. There are several disadvantages of recording during the assessment interview:

1. The interviewer's writing tends to distract the child from their task of solving problems.
2. The interviewer is distracted from posing tasks, and carefully observing and determining the child's strategies.
3. The interview takes more time.
4. The interviewer tends to focus on eliciting responses that can be easily recorded.

5. The interviewer tends to focus too much on whether the child is correct or incorrect and to record observations in terms of correctness of responses.

Teaching to the Test

In the development of MR the label 'teaching to the test' was used to describe a tendency of a small minority of MR teachers to focus instruction specifically on items on the MR Assessment Schedule. This involved presenting their MR child with tasks on the MR Assessment Schedule, and having their child frequently practise solving the tasks, for example in each teaching session. This practice is at odds with the purpose of MR, which is to advance the child's knowledge across a wide range of early number content. The MR assessment procedure involves a process of sampling the child's knowledge and strategies from various areas of content. Each assessment task can be regarded as being representative of a large group of possible tasks. Clearly, the notion of tasks being representative is less realistic if children are continually practising the assessment tasks. On the other hand, it is not necessary for teachers to deliberately avoid presenting tasks from the MR Assessment Schedule, for example in cases where such a task is part of a coherent teaching sequence. Examples of teaching to the test are: (1) training children to correctly name the regular or irregular arrays on Task Group 3, that is, the subitizing tasks; and (2) using, in MR instruction, the cards used in Task Group 12, that is, the uncovering tasks.

Independent Validation of Assessment Interviews

This is the process whereby assessment interviews, as well as being analysed by the interviewer or a colleague, are also analysed independently by a validator. This is an important aspect of the MR Programme and accordingly is undertaken by an especially trained and experienced person. It is important to realize that validation of assessment does not lessen the importance of skilful and comprehensive interviewing during assessment. The validator has no information available beyond the videotaped interview. Thus it is important in the assessment process that the interviewer works strenuously and skilfully to elicit the child's most advanced strategies. This involves persistence and ensuring that supplementary tasks are used when necessary.

Issues in Teaching

Microadjusting

In MR we have seen many examples of teachers skilfully using the technique of microadjusting. Typically in these examples, significant learning on the part of the child is very apparent. The technique of microadjusting is central to MR teaching, and was mentioned in the Introduction (p. 5). MR sessions are intended to be highly interactive in that the teacher is constantly monitoring and taking account of the child's problem-solving and learning. Thus each task posed by the teacher is informed by the teacher's observation and reflection of the child's prior activity. The teacher has a hypothesized model or view of the child's current knowledge and strategies, and is constantly adjusting and elaborating (i.e. extending) her model. Each new task is judged by the teacher to be optimal in some sense. This sense of being optimal is somewhat complex in that it embraces both a sufficient degree of difficulty or challenge and a reasonable likelihood of success. Additionally, the new task takes account of a particular learning goal, that is, a likely construction on the part of the child, determined by the teacher. Mathematics Recovery teaching as it is intended to be, that is, highly interactive, problem based and embracing microadjusting, is akin to what is known as Socratic teaching. Experience with MR teachers has indicated that the technique of microadjusting can be developed through practice, reflection and peer and leader discussion. An illustration of microadjusting in response to the child's ongoing success in solving the tasks follows below.

An Illustration of Microadjusting

The teacher is using a setting involving bundles of tens and ones. The teacher has determined that incrementing by tens and ones is a reasonable goal for the child. At some point in the teaching sequence the teacher displays two bundles of ten and asks the child how many sticks there are. The child answers 'twenty'. The teacher then screens the two bundles, places out another bundle which remains unscreened and asks the child how many sticks there are altogether. The child says, 'twenty, thirty!' The teacher then puts the three bundles together, and briefly displays and then screens them. She then places out a ten and two ones and asks the child how many altogether. The child answers, 'thirty, forty, forty-one, forty-two!' The teacher now presents a task involving two screened collections rather than one screened and one unscreened. In posing the next task the teacher briefly displays and then screens four bundles of ten, and then briefly displays and then screens two bundles of ten. The child answers 'forty, fifty, sixty!'. The teacher now decides to present a task in which both collections are screened, and the second collection has both tens and ones. In the instructional sequence just described, the teacher has made several microadjustments on the basis of her ongoing observations of the child's responses.

Transitional Tasks

In the early phases of MR a teaching technique was developed that came to be known as using a transitional task. This was especially useful in situations where a child seemed to have no means of solving a particular type of task or seemed to have little comprehension of the task. This technique involved devising a type of task that was simpler than but closely related to the original type of task. A transitional task used successfully in the case of Missing Addend tasks involved displaying a collection of, say, six counters and asking the child to put out more counters in order to make nine altogether. The technique of using a transitional task can be regarded as a particularly creative form of microadjusting.

Modelling and Scaffolding

In MR, the issue of modelling as an teaching technique has arisen frequently. For many of the MR teachers, modelling is a technique that is prominent in early literacy and thus it is natural that they should consider its relevance in early number work. In MR we take modelling to mean demonstrating a strategy to the child. Thus the teacher might demonstrate the strategy of counting-on to solve an additive problem, and have the child imitate the teacher. Modelling in this sense is closely aligned to the technique of 'scaffolding' which is also prominent in early literacy. We take scaffolding in early number work to mean the teacher providing some of the steps of a solution strategy in order to assist the child. Thus, whereas modelling involves demonstrating the whole strategy, scaffolding involves providing one or two initial steps of the strategy. In MR, modelling is not advocated as a routine instructional technique. This is because modelling is not consistent with the guiding principles of the problem-based approach to teaching in MR. In MR instruction, the teacher's task is to pose a task that is within the child's range and which the child is likely to solve after a reasonable amount of effort and concentration. Excessive use of modelling may result in situations where the child expects to learn by imitating the teacher.

Scaffolding, Modelling and Microadjusting

Mathematics Recovery teachers have used techniques that are akin to scaffolding. Consider a scenario where a teacher is presenting Missing Addend tasks to a child and the child does not seem to have any means to solve the tasks. This is a relatively common occurrence in MR. The child does not seem to comprehend the task and may respond by attempting to add the two given numbers or by randomly guessing. As an example, the teacher uses screened counters to present the Missing Addend task of '6 to 9', that is, six and how many more to make nine, and the child simply guesses or tries to add 6 and 9. Three ways that the teacher might proceed are:

1. Modelling, for example demonstrate the procedure of counting-up-to and have the child imitate the procedure.
2. Scaffolding, for example demonstrate the first step of the procedure of counting-up-to, for example 'seven is one more' and have the child try to complete the solution.
3. Microadjusting, for example pose a new missing addend task that is judged to be more likely to be solved by the child using counting-up-to, for example '6 to 7'.

Of the three examples just given, (3) is the one most in accordance with the guiding principles.

Child Self-Checking

Child self-checking has a very important role in MR assessment and teaching. An important principle is that children should routinely use an appropriate means of checking, and in checking situations, teachers should advance as little information as possible. Thus to the extent possible, the actions and decisions in checking should be those of the child rather than the teacher. The various additive and subtractive tasks used in MR are particularly suited to checking. As an example, a child who solves an additive task involving two screened collections can be asked to remove the screens and check their solution by counting the displayed items. The decision on the basis of the check, of whether the child was correct in their initial solution, should also be left to the child. Thus when the child has completed checking the teacher might ask, 'Were you correct?' When children are encouraged to check in this way checking can become an almost routine procedure undertaken after solving a problem. Children can begin to appreciate the idea of verification or proof, which is an important and general idea in mathematics.

Mathematics Recovery teachers have reported that children seemed to gain a good deal of satisfaction through checking for themselves that their answer is correct, after solving a problem. Thus checking seemed to positively influence the child's attitude as well as their learning. When checking is approached in this way the child becomes less dependent on the teacher. Experience has shown that children can be highly motivated in situations where teachers provide little or no feedback to children about the correctness of their solutions and where children routinely check their solutions, that is, by using a less advanced strategy. The children's motivation can be attributed to intrinsic satisfaction from solving challenging problems and confirming the solutions, and the unstated recognition on the part of teacher and child that this is happening.

Should Teachers Ever Tell Children Answers?

The issue of whether teachers should tell a child the answer to a mathematical problem that the child has not been able to solve is one that often arises in discussions of constructivist approaches to teaching mathematics. For some, any act of telling children an answer is at odds with constructivist principles because the child is denied the opportunity of constructing or inventing knowledge. The view taken in MR teaching is that telling can be productive in some situations. For example, in cases where children seem to particularly want to know a solution to a problem that they have been trying to solve, it would seem appropriate and desirable to tell the child the solution. Knowledge in the form of a solution that is told to the child, rather than the child having solved a problem to obtain the solution, can be of value to children. In very general terms, telling as an instructional technique has a long and successful history – people learn a lot of what they know from being told. Smith (1996) provides an extensive discussion of issues related to teaching mathematics by telling and the tension between this and current reform efforts in mathematics education.

In early number, children may subsequently make use of knowledge in the form of answers that are told to them. Nevertheless, the teacher should keep in mind that in situations where they have told the child an answer, there may be significant limitations on the child's knowledge. Thus it is unlikely that the child understands a solution as a consequence of being told, in the same way that a child does who arrives at the answer by solving a problem. In many cases in MR teaching, where a child cannot solve a problem there is an obvious alternative to telling. This involves the teacher in microadjusting their teaching.

For example, the teacher might change some of the circumstances of the problem so that it essentially becomes a new and simpler problem, but it is the 'same' problem in the sense that it has the same answer. In the case of an additive task with one collection screened, the teacher might unscreen one of the two collections.

Role of Notating and Symbolizing in MR

In the early phases of MR much of the teaching focused on children's verbally based strategies. Mathematics Recovery teachers raised several issues concerning a need to take close account of the realities of the mathematics classrooms of the participants. One of these issues was the written mathematics of the classroom. It seemed that in MR sessions, children were progressing in terms of developing more sophisticated verbally based strategies. At the same time much of their classroom mathematics involved written number work, typically within a specific range of numbers, for example numbers to 20. A consequence of this was that some children were progressing in MR teaching sessions but this progress was not always reflected in their classroom mathematics. In order to address this, it was decided that, for children who had advanced to Stage 3, that is, they were spontaneously counting-on to solve additive and Missing Addend tasks, there would be a focus on mathematical notation and symbolizing as well as verbally based strategies. This involved drawing on research by Cobb and colleagues (Cobb *et al.*, 1995; Cobb *et al.*, 1997a; Cobb *et al.*, 1997b). The focus on notating and symbolizing involves teachers guiding children to find ways to express their verbally based strategies in symbolic form. Thus the resulting mathematical notation arises from and accords with the child's verbally based strategies. Use of notation and symbolizing in this way can serve two purposes. First, it can provide a basis for children to become more familiar with the written number work of their classroom mathematics. Second, the notational systems that children develop and use can provide a basis through which their numerical knowledge can be advanced. In traditional approaches to early number teaching, typically children are introduced to standard or adult forms of notation and expected to understand and use these from the outset. In contrast, in this approach there is a protracted period during which children initially use methods that accord with their verbally based strategies. These methods are progressively modified and made more concise, thus providing a basis for understanding and using standard, adult forms.

Children's Solution Strategies: Certitude, Robustness, Spontaneity
Certitude, robustness and spontaneity are important features of children's solution strategies, and it is necessary for the MR teacher to be aware of and take account of these in MR assessment and teaching.

Certitude
Consider, as an example, a child who uses counting-on to solve the addition task of 7 + 4 involving two screened collections. Certitude relates to the extent to which the child has certainty, sureness or confidence in their solution. One child may consider the problem to be very routine and be very confident about the answer, while to another child the problem may have been a substantial one and they may have little or no confidence in their solution. For some children 8 – 6 is a very challenging problem and they may arrive at the answer 'two' with little or no certitude. For these children checking or explaining 8 – 6 = 2 is a genuine problem. For other children the task of 8 – 6 is very straightforward or even trivial. Paradoxically, these children often find it difficult to check or explain 8 – 6 = 2. Questioning the answer does not make sense to them. There are various means by which the MR teacher can get a sense of the child's certitude with a particular strategy. An obvious approach is to simply ask the child, for example, 'Are your sure?' This can work well provided it is not used so frequently that the child develops a routine response to the question. Another good indicator of certitude is the facility displayed by the child in solving the problem. The child who answers immediately or quickly counts on to solve the problem is likely to be more confident with their answer than the child who takes a long time to commence counting-on and proceeds hesitantly.

Robustness
Robustness refers to the extent to which the child can use the strategy on similar problems. Consider the strategy of counting-on to solve additive or Missing Addend tasks. The child who can use counting-on only in the range one to ten, and can only count-on one or two counts does not have a robust counting-on strategy. The child who can count on from any number to 100 and beyond, and can keep track of up to six counts, has a much more robust strategy.

Spontaneity
Spontaneity refers to the child generating the strategy on their own, that is, in the absence of direct or indirect assistance from the teacher

or from special circumstances inherent to the problem and solution attempt. Counting-on is spontaneous when the child uses the strategy without any obvious assistance. Assessment and teaching situations in which the child's solution is not spontaneous can be useful because they can result in novel awareness on the child's part of a particular strategy. There are many instances in MR where, in the first instance, a strategy has arisen non-spontaneously, and following this the child learns to use the strategy spontaneously.

Instructional Goals for the Child Who is Counting-On (i.e. at Stage 3)

Mathematics Recovery participants are typically assessed at Stages 0, 1 or 2 on SEAL. Particularly in the case of Stage 2 children, teachers pragmatically adopted the goal of advancing these children to Stage 3, which is characterized by counting-on to solve additive and subtractive tasks. In some cases teachers were able to achieve this goal in several weeks, at which point they adopted the goal of advancing the child to Stage 4, characterized by counting-down-to. On the basis of work with several children we began to question the appropriateness of setting Stage 4 as an instructional goal for children who had attained Stage 3. The goal of developing counting-down-to seemed too narrow and some children did not spontaneously use counting-down-to when they might be expected to do so. We also encountered difficulty in finding a range of instructional settings and tasks in which the strategy of counting-down-to was likely to arise. For this reason it was decided to set Stage 5 as the instructional goal for children who had developed counting-on as a robust and spontaneous strategy. We were able to determine a range of instructional settings and tasks that were appropriate for Stage 3 children, and at the same time, seemed likely to build a basis of knowledge for Stage 5. Children advance beyond Stage 4 without it being a specific teaching goal.

Learning Pathways to Stage 5 of SEAL

In the first year of the project we adopted the view that children would advance to Stage 5 of SEAL (see Chapter 4) via the development of advanced count-by-ones strategies and that it was important in MR teaching to use settings and tasks that were likely to result in the development of these strategies. At the same time we became more aware of the potential of other aspects of early numerical knowledge, for example combining and partitioning and base-five, to provide a basis for the development of Stage 5 strategies, that is, non-count-by-ones strategies. Thus, for the child at Stage 2, teaching could have as its immediate goal, either the development of advanced counting strategies or the development of knowledge in the aspects of combining and partitioning and base-five.

In MR we have adopted the view that, for any child, there are several possible paths of learning by which the child might advance from, for example, Stage 2 to Stage 5, and that the child's particular path will be strongly determined by the settings and tasks used. Thus teaching might: (1) include prominent use of settings to present additive and subtractive tasks, for example screened collections, with the goal of developing advanced counting strategies; (2) emphasize the development of combining and partitioning and base-five and base-ten strategies; (3) include prominent use of settings and tasks involving spatial patterns; or (4) include some combination of two or all three of these. An important question is the extent to which certain children might be better served by a particular emphasis.

Instruction on Backward Number Word Sequences (BNWSs)

An often asked question about MR is why there is an emphasis on BNWSs as well as FNWSs. This question arises for two main reasons. First, in much of the current curricula and practice there is little or no emphasis on BNWSs and, second, in general terms focusing on BNWSs is not regarded as necessary or important in children's learning of subtraction. Some writers have argued that in teaching subtraction, children should be taught to use a counting-on strategy rather than counting back. There are several points that can be made in support of emphasizing BNWSs as well as FNWSs in the teaching of early number. First, able children typically have well-developed knowledge of BNWSs as well as FNWSs, whereas less able children have little or no knowledge of BNWSs. This provides a justification for emphasizing BNWSs in MR, because the knowledge of and strategies used by able children can provide teachers with a useful guide to planning for less able children.

Second, when a problem-based approach is taken to instruction in which children develop strategies in their attempts to solve problems, children invariably use strategies involving counting-down. When solving a task such as $15 - 2$, for example, a child who is not at Stage 5, has little choice but to solve the problem by counting back two counts. Clearly, this is easier for the child than counting forward from 2 to 15 or backward from 15 to 2, and keeping track of the number of counts. Thus in an approach in which children's spontaneous strategies are valued and encouraged, it seems appropriate to empha-size BNWSs in the likely event that children attempt to use BNWSs in solving subtractive problems.

Instructional Materials and Real-World Problems

In MR teaching, simple, practical materials such as counters, numeral cards, Numeral Tracks, etc. have been observed to work well in terms of children being motivated to solve problems. Using these materials has resulted in significant progress for children and thus there is no reason to believe that more elaborate materials and real-world sce-narios are essential for successful learning. Children do not seem to be bored by or lack motivation to attempt to solve tasks that were purely numerical rather than real-world in the sense of involving some everyday situation that was determined to be of special interest to the child. An interesting aspect of this was that some observers argued that the materials used in MR were not sufficiently interesting for chil-dren and, in similar vein, argued that the tasks would prove boring for children. In practice, there was little or no evidence to support these arguments.

In our experience it was not necessary to cast all numerical prob-lems as everyday situations in order to make them understandable or of interest to children. Children seemed equally happy completing a task based on number word sequences, numeral sequences or coun-ters, etc. This led us to question the extent to which word problems and everyday situations were central to children's numerical learning.

Motivation and Challenge in Early Number Learning

While some observers argued that the materials and tasks used in MR would be boring for children (see previous section), others argued that having children attempt to solve numerical tasks that were difficult for them would result in negative attitudes to mathematics on the part of the children. The experience from the programme is quite at odds with this claim. There are many examples where children undergo sustained hard thinking, for example for periods of 30 seconds to one minute, when attempting to solve a problem. There are also many instances where children seem particularly satisfied by their efforts to solve dif-ficult problems. Thus in teaching situations where tasks are chosen judiciously in order to be within the child's ability range (the zone of proximal development in Vygotsky's terms), working with challenging and difficult tasks seems to result in strong positive motivation on the part of children. The proviso to this is that the child experiences a reasonable amount of success in problem-solving.

These points constitute a challenge to traditional views held by some, that a range of elaborate materials, manipulation of materials by children, and use of scenarios involving everyday situations are important for learning and necessary to ensure motivation and positive attitudes. The experience in MR is that having children solve challenging problems, that is, problems that are closely tailored to their current levels of learning, can be an important motivational factor. Thus children can gain intrinsic motivation from hard thinking and the knowledge that they are progressing in their learning.

Variability in Instructional Materials

This issue concerns the extent to which it is necessary or desirable to use a range of materials to teach a particular mathematical idea. For example, when initially teaching the idea of addition to what extent is it important for children to use several different kinds of manipulative materials? The notion that using a range of materials is important, has been labelled the variability principle and has been advocated by some writers in early mathematics education, notably Zoltan Dienes. Thus it is not surprising that teachers would subscribe to this principle, and such teachers were included among those participating in the MR Programme.

In broad terms the argument in favour of the principle is that the child is more likely to, in a sense, abstract the mathematical idea from the range of materials being used, than from just one material. The instructional approach in MR emphasizes the child constructing knowledge through problem-solving and reflection. In this approach it has not been necessary to adopt the variability principle. A different but related issue is the question of whether an MR child is more suited to one particular material or setting than another. Thus, using a wide range of settings might be justified not because variability is considered desirable for its own sake but, rather, because it is thought that some settings might be more conducive to a particular child's learning than other settings. In class teaching, if one believes that particular children may be more suited to particular settings and materials, then using a range of materials is likely to suit a larger number of children than using only one material or setting.

Issues

Questioning the Lock-Step Curriculum

In traditional approaches to teaching early number, the curriculum was organized into a strict sequence of topics. According to this sequence the kindergarten year focused on numbers to 10, and in first-grade this was extended to numbers to 20, etc. Also, in number work beyond 10, place value was regarded as a strict learning prerequisite for addition and subtraction. Mathematics Recovery has challenged this lock-step approach in several ways. First, kindergarteners and reception children are no longer largely limited to working in the range 1 to 10. Rather, as soon as feasible, teaching for these children includes number word sequences and numerals to 100 and beyond, as well as numbers in the range 1 to 10. Many participating teachers have expressed surprise or amazement at the success of these approaches. In similar vein, Year 1 are taught to name and sequence two- and three-digit numerals and to work with FNWSs and BNWSs well beyond 20.

In MR, teaching Year 1 the place value of numbers in the teens and numbers beyond 20 is not regarded as a prerequisite for addition or subtraction. The view taken is that kindergarten and Year 1 children can and should solve additive and subtractive tasks involving combinations of a number in the teens and a single-digit number (e.g. 13 + 4, 16 − 3), long before they understand the tens and ones structure of teen numbers. Similarly they should solve tasks involving a two-digit number and a single-digit number (e.g. 26 + 5, 87 + x = 92, 42 − 4) long before understanding place value of two-digit numbers. Typically these problems are presented verbally rather than in written form. Children's early strategies for adding and subtracting are typically verbally based and do not involve an explicit awareness of place value. Thus, for example, the child might use a verbal strategy, for example counting-on to add six on to 19 without any awareness that 19 consists of one ten and nine ones, or might subtract four from 83 without awareness of the tens and ones structure of numbers in the eighties. In similar vein, children might use a verbal strategy to add two two-digit numbers before they fully understand two-digit place value. Using verbal strategies to add and subtract in this way can constitute a means through which place value is learned. Thus rather than being a prerequisite to addition and subtraction, place value should be learned in conjunction with addition and subtraction.

Skills-Based and Constructivist Approaches

A question frequently asked about MR is: is it a skills-based pro-gramme? This question is taken as asking whether the major focus of the programme is developing children's number skills, where the term number skills is used in a relatively narrow sense, for example habit-uation of number facts, mastery of standard algorithms, etc. Inter-preted in this sense the answer to the question is 'no' but this should not be taken as an indication that in the programme number skills are regarded as unimportant in early number learning. Because the pro-gramme includes emphasis on aspects such as facility with number word sequences and Numeral Identification it may appear at first glance to be a somewhat narrowly focused skills-based programme. It is certainly the case that, in the programme, it is considered impor-tant to document the extent of the child's knowledge of specific aspects such as FNWS, BNWS and Numeral Identification. Further, it is quite typical for teaching objectives to include developing the child's knowl-edge in these aspects. Nevertheless, it is quite misleading to charac-terize the programme as skills based in a narrow sense.

As stated in earlier chapters, the theoretical bases of MR are con-structivist research programmes in early number learning conducted in the 1980s and 1990s. These research programmes focused on understanding the strategies children use to solve problems in early number and how those strategies develop over time. The current pro-gramme reflects many important aspects of these earlier research pro-grammes. The guiding framework, that is, LFIN, results from the earlier constructivist research as does the emphasis in assessment on understanding and documenting the child's numerical strategies. The problem-based approach to teaching, as detailed in the Introduction (see 'Guiding Principles for MR Teaching'), also results directly from approaches which were used in the earlier research. The approach in MR is enquiry based or problem based rather than skills based. The teaching approach emphasizes learning through problem-solving and reflection, and teachers being explicitly aware of and taking account of children's solution strategies.

Children's Attitudes in MR

The vast majority of MR participants seem to have a very positive attitude to participating in the programme. Mathematics Recovery teachers have reported many instances where children initially seemed shy and uncertain about their participation and changed dramatically for the better after a few weeks in the programme. Typically these changes were noticed by the classroom teacher and parents as well as the MR teacher, that is, these changes were accompanied by similar changes in the child's approach to classroom tasks and in the home. Mathematics Recovery teaching sessions involved children in prolonged periods of concentration and they seemed to thrive on solving challenging problems. For these children, the key ingredients for developing a positive attitude were that they were challenged with difficult tasks requiring sustained effort, they were generally successful in solving the instructional tasks and they were aware that they were making progress in their number learning. Mathematics Recovery teachers did encounter a minority of children who did not seem to have a positive attitude to participation. In the vast majority of cases there were external circumstances that were likely to be the cause of significant attitudinal difficulties.

In some of the schools in which MR was implemented the view was expressed by some teachers that the act of withdrawing children for mathematics instruction could result in negative attitude on the part of the children. Examples were cited of remedial classes in mathematics where these types of reactions on the part of participants were a common occurrence. There is no indication in MR that participants have a negative attitude to withdrawal and participation, and this is likely to be attributable to MR participants being younger than children in other withdrawal programmes and being withdrawn individually rather than as a member of a group.

By way of contrast there are many instances in MR where children spontaneously seem to be particularly happy to participate. In similar vein, many children express displeasure at being discontinued in MR. Mathematics Recovery participants seem to enjoy working one to one with an adult in a cognitively supportive environment. It seems that working in this way for an extended period on a daily basis, and succeeding at difficult problem-solving, constitutes a very positive experience and for many children, a rare or at least infrequent experience.

Increasing Number Awareness

As a final point, MR teachers have frequently reported that their children had developed an increasing awareness of numbers as a result of their participation in MR. This had occurred without any particular efforts by MR teachers to make children more aware of numbers around them. Thus the positive attitudes of MR children to number work was often accompanied by increasing number awareness.

Length of MR Teaching Cycles

In the first two years of the development of MR, teaching cycles were of 16 hours' duration except in the case of a few children who left the programme earlier because they changed schools. By and large the participants in the first two years were able to make substantial progress. Since 1994, teaching cycles have ranged up to 40 hours. The current approach taken in MR is that teaching cycles should be of 20 to 24 hours' length, but longer cycles may be used if there seems to be a sound case for doing so. Children who clearly have progressed to average or above average levels relative to their class may be discontinued earlier than the twentieth hour of their teaching cycle. Experience has shown that children who have not made some reasonable progress by the twelfth hour of the teaching cycle are not likely to make progress overall. For this reason a review of the progress of each MR participant after twelve hours of teaching is advocated. A participant who has clearly progressed in terms of performance in teaching sessions need not be reassessed at this point. A child for whom there is very little or no progress should be discontinued and their progress or lack of progress should be determined via a final assessment.

Attainment Level for Successful Discontinuation

In general terms a participant should be discontinued when they have reached a level at which they are likely to succeed with regular classroom teaching. This has typically been interpreted as reaching an average or above average level for their class. This might be determined by (1) informally comparing the children's performance level in MR teaching sessions with classroom performance levels that typify a class average; (2) assessing one or more children whom the class teacher judges to be representative of an average level for the class; or (3) giving an MR assessment to all of the children in the class or school to determine their levels on each of the MR models, and thereby determining median (i.e. middle) levels. Clearly, (1) is the least time-consuming and (3) is the most. An additional benefit of undertaking (3) is that it provides a comprehensive picture of all the children in the cohort, and for this reason it is worth doing occasionally if not routinely.

Summary

This chapter has focused on issues in MR assessment and teaching. Issues in assessment include the outcomes of assessment, variability among MR participants, purpose of videotaping, revisiting assessment tasks, taking a flexible approach to assessment, reasons for not recording during the interview, teaching to the test, and independent validation of assessment interviews.

Issues in teaching include microadjusting, modelling and scaffolding, child self-checking, telling children answers, the role of notating and symbolizing, aspects of children's solution strategies such as certitude, robustness and spontaneity, teaching objectives for the child who is counting-on, learning paths to Stage 5 of SEAL, instruction on BNWSs, practical materials and real-world problems, motivation and challenge in number learning, and variability in instructional materials. Programmatic issues include questioning the lock-step curriculum, skills-based and constructivist approaches, children's attitudes in MR, length of MR teaching cycles and attainment level for successful discontinuation.

9

Extending the Learning Framework to Multiplication and Division

Robert J. Wright, Joanne Mulligan and Peter Gould

This chapter includes:

- an overview of the development of children's early multiplication and division knowledge and strategies;
- an associated model consisting of five levels;
- for each level, an explanation and an illustration in the form of a protocol of a child's solutions of multiplicative or divisional tasks;
- an assessment schedule for early multiplication and division knowledge and strategies;
- summary guidelines for determining levels of early multiplication and division knowledge;
- five scenarios for which the reader is challenged to identify the child's level and solutions and explanations for the scenarios; and
- exemplary instructional tasks for early multiplication and division.

Development of Early Multiplication and Division Knowledge and Strategies

In the Count Me In Too project in Australia, recent work has been undertaken to extend the Learning Framework in Number in order to include a focus on children's early multiplication and division knowledge. This work has drawn on an extensive range of current research in this area (see Mulligan, 1998).

Children's early multiplication and division knowledge and strategies result from cognitive reorganizations of their counting, addition and subtraction strategies. Thus, for young children, multiplication and division knowledge and strategies build on counting, addition, subtraction and also number word sequences, and combining and partitioning. Children's early multiplication knowledge and early division knowledge are interrelated and are also closely linked with addition and subtraction strategies, and early fraction learning. Thus the development of combining and partitioning strategies as well as early arithmetical strategies involving counting, addition and subtraction, can form an important basis for the development of multiplication and division strategies. Various aspects of multiplication and division can be seen as overlapping with, or building on, these strategies. Thus two or more situations involving multiplication and division may involve similar counting and other strategies.

However, it has long been recognized that multiplication is not simply a process of repeated addition, and that division is not simply a process of sharing. Multiplication and division knowledge differs from addition and subtraction mainly because the former incorporates the ability to use equal groups as 'abstract composite units' (Steffe, 1992b): 'An abstract composite unit [is] the result of applying the integration operation to a numerical composite or to a symbolized numerical composite. The child focuses on the unit structure of a numerical composite e.g. one ten, rather than on the unit items e.g. ten ones' (Steffe and Cobb, 1988, p. 334). In the case of multiplication or division an abstract composite unit is a collection of items that is viewed as one thing. For example, a child for whom three is an abstract composite unit can regard three items as 'one three'. The child can also regard three items as 'three ones'. That this is so follows from the description of an abstract composite unit given above, because an abstract composite unit is a cognitive advancement on a numerical composite.

The child who has advanced multiplication and division knowledge can conceptualize a group of equal groups as a composite of composites. In the case of three sixes, for example, the child is aware of three as a composite unit and at the same time, aware of each of the groups of six as a composite unit. 'For a situation to be established as multiplicative, it is necessary at least to co-ordinate two composite units in such a way that one of the composite units is distributed over elements of the other composite unit' (Steffe, 1994, p. 19). Thus a framework of the development of multiplication and division knowledge should account for the acquisition of a cognitive structure based on equal grouping which is at the heart of multiplicative reasoning (Anghileri, 1989; Confrey, 1994; Kouba, 1989; Steffe, 1992b).

Research shows that children as young as 4 or 5 years old can solve simple multiplicative and divisional tasks by using materials and counting. Studies show that young children can develop multiplication and division concepts in the first years of schooling and highlight that teaching practices may not necessarily focus on children's potential mathematical development (Carpenter *et al.*, 1993; Clark and Kamii,

1996; Hunting, Davis and Pearn, 1996; Kouba, 1989; Mulligan and Mitchelmore, 1997). On the other hand, there is growing evidence that once children reach the primary (elementary) grades (i.e. the fourth year of school and around eight years of age) many are unable to solve problems involving multiplication and division or apply multiplicative number facts with meaning. Children need to be presented with specific problem-based situations designed to encourage the construction of abstract composite units. This will promote a range of increasingly sophisticated strategies based on counting in multiples, and addition and subtraction. This is a necessary phase for children before they acquire facile strategies for multiplying and dividing and, related to this, 'automatized' basic fact knowledge.

Children may use identical or very similar strategies for solving both multiplicative and divisional tasks except that, in the case of division, the child will form and count composite units based on a given divisor. Interestingly, it has been found that division is not necessarily more difficult than multiplication and, in many cases, a divisional task may be easier than a corresponding multiplicative task. For example, it may be easier for a child to share counters into equal groups and count the number of groups rather than keep track of a larger number of composite groups as is necessary in the case of multiplication. Research indicates that teaching children to share and group small numbers into equal parts can facilitate the development of relatively sophisticated multiplication and division strategies, that is, strategies more advanced than counting by ones.

In this chapter a model of early multiplication and division knowledge consisting of five levels is explained. Links between this model and the SEAL model (Chapter 4) should be very apparent to the reader: the notions of numerical composites, abstract composite units and composites of composites are central features of the model of early multiplication and division knowledge, and the first two of these are also central to the SEAL model, because Stage 3 and Stage 5 are characterized by the construction of numerical composites and abstract composite units respectively.

Model of the Development of Early Multiplication and Division Knowledge

Table 9.1 outlines a progression of five levels in children's development of early multiplication and division knowledge. The model is adapted from that developed by Mulligan (1998) and used in the Count Me In Too project (NSW Department of Education and Training, 1998).

Table 9.1 Model for early multiplication and division levels

Level 1: Initial Grouping. Uses perceptual counting (i.e. by ones) to establish the numerosity of a collection of equal groups, to share items into groups of a given size (quotitive sharing), and to share items into a given number of groups (partitive sharing).

Level 2: Perceptual Counting in Multiples. Uses a multiplicative counting strategy to count visible items arranged in equal groups.

Level 3: Figurative Composite Grouping. Uses a multiplicative counting strategy to count items arranged in equal groups in cases where the individual items are not visible.

Level 4: Repeated Abstract Composite Grouping. Counts composite units in repeated addition or subtraction, that is, uses the composite unit a specified number of times.

Level 5: Multiplication and Division as Operations. Can regard both the number in each group and the number of groups as a composite unit. Can immediately recall or quickly derive many of the basic facts for multiplication and division.

Explaining the Levels of Early Multiplication and Division Knowledge

In this section each of the five levels of early multiplication and division knowledge is explained and illustrated via a video excerpt that describes a child's solution of one or more multiplicative or divisional tasks.

Level 1: Initial Grouping

The child at Level 1 can establish the numerosity of a collection of equal groups when the items are visible and counts by ones when doing so, that is, the child uses perceptual counting (see Stage 1 of SEAL in Chapter 4). The child can make groups of a specified size from a collection of items, for example given 12 counters the child can arrange the counters into groups of three thereby obtaining four groups. This is referred to as quotitive sharing, and is also known as the grouping aspect of division. The child can also share a collection of items into a specified number of groups, for example given 20 counters the child can share the counters into five equal groups. This is referred to as partitive sharing and is also known as the sharing aspect of division. The child does not count in multiples.

Video Excerpt 1: Kim and Beau

At the beginning of his interview Beau arranged 18 counters into groups of three obtaining six groups. He also shared 20 counters into five equal groups. In each of these tasks Beau was asked to count the total number of counters, and he counted by ones to do so. The interview continued as follows:

K: Can you count by twos for me and I'll tell you when to stop.

B: (Extends two fingers on his right hand. Points over the desk with his two extended fingers in co-ordination with each number word.) Two, four, six, eight, ten, (looks towards Kim) twelve.

K: Can you go any further?

B: (Shakes his head.) Umm, no.

K: Can you count by fives for me?

B: Yep. (Extends five fingers on his right hand.) Umm – (touches the desk with his right hand in co-ordination with each number word) ten, twenty (softly) I think, umm – .

K: Try counting by fives this time. Five – .

B: (Counts slowly and touches the desk in co-ordination with each count.) Five, ten, umm (looks at Kim) seven?

K: Stop there. Try counting by threes for me and I'll tell you when to stop.

B: (Extends three fingers on his right hand. Counts slowly and touches the desk in co-ordination with each count.) Ten, twenty, thirty – , umm ten – .

K: Okay, stop there. (Places out five rows of three counters arranged in a 5 × 3 array.) Can you count by threes this time and tell me how many counters are there?

B: (Places a finger on each counter in the first row and then the second row in co-ordination with counting.) Ten, twenty – . Can you count by tens?

K: Can you count by threes?

B: (As before, places fingers on counters in the first row and then the second row.) Three, ten – (looks at Kim).

K: Okay, stop there.

Discussion of Video Excerpt 1

Beau could produce the number word sequence of multiples of two, up to twelve. But he could not produce multiples of five or three. When asked to count a 5 × 3 array of counters by threes, he was unable to do so. Beau was able to share collections of counters into groups of a specified size and into a given number of equal groups, and when doing so counted the total number of counters by ones. Beau's strategies are indicative of Level I, that is, Initial Grouping.

Level 2: Perceptual Counting in Multiples

The child at Level 2 has developed counting strategies that are more advanced than those used in Level 1. These multiplicative counting strategies involve implicitly or explicitly counting in multiples. After sharing a collection into equal groups the child uses one of these strategies to count all the items contained in the groups, which are necessarily visible. The child is not able to count the items in situations where the groups are screened. These counting strategies include rhythmic, double and skip counting, and each is given the label 'perceptual' (e.g. perceptual rhythmic counting) because of the child's reliance on visible items.

Strategies for Counting in Multiples (Multiplicative Counting Strategies)

Rhythmic counting involves counting all the items contained in several equal groups by ones and emphasizing the number word reached after each group is counted, for example when counting three groups of four the child emphasizes 'four', 'eight' and 'twelve', that is, 'one, two, three, *four*', etc. Double counting in the context of early multiplication or division involves counting all the items contained in several equal groups by ones in co-ordination with counting the number of groups by ones, for example 'one, two, three, four – one; five, six, seven, eight – two', etc. Skip counting involves counting by threes, fours, etc. when counting all the items contained in several equal groups.

Video Excerpt 2: Sarah and Delise

At the beginning of her interview Delise arranged 16 counters into groups of two obtaining eight groups. She also shared 30 counters into six equal groups. When asked to count the total number of counters Delise counted by twos to sixteen on the first task and by fives to thirty on the second task. The interview continued as follows:

S: Count by fives and I'll tell you when to stop.

D: Five, ten, fifteen, (pauses briefly) twenty, twenty-five, (pauses briefly) thirty, thirty-five, forty.

S: Stop there please. This time count by threes and I'll tell you when to stop.

D: Three, six, nine, (after two seconds) twelve, (after three seconds) fifteen.

S: Okay stop there please. (Places out six rows of three counters arranged in a 6 × 3 array.) Can you count by threes and tell me how many counters are there?

D: (Points to each row in turn.) Three, six, nine, (pauses briefly) twelve, fifteen, (after two seconds) eighteen!

Discussion of Video Excerpt 2

Delise could produce the number word sequence of multiples of five, up to forty, and the number word sequence of multiples of three up to fifteen. She also counted by threes to establish the numerosity of a 6 × 3 array of counters and, in similar vein, counted by twos to sixteen and by fives to thirty on tasks involving collections of counters that she had arranged into equal groups. Delise's strategies are indicative of Level 2, that is, Perceptual Counting in Multiples.

Level 3: Figurative Composite Grouping

The child at Level 3 has developed counting strategies that do not rely on items being visible and which do not involve counting by ones. For example, if the child is presented with four groups of three counters, where each group is separately screened, the child may use skip counting by threes to determine the number of counters in all, that is, 'three, six, nine, twelve'. From the child's perspective each of the four screens symbolizes a collection of three items but the individual items are not visible. There is a correspondence between not having to count by ones on tasks involving equal groups and counting-on in the case of an additive task, for example 6 + 3 presented with two screened collections. In the case of the additive task the first screen symbolizes the collection of six counters and the child does not need to count from one to six. Thus one would expect children at Level 3 in terms of early multiplication and division to have attained Stage 3 in terms of SEAL.

Video Excerpt 3: Anna and Jenna

A: (Places out six containers.) Jenna I have six containers here. (Takes one container and empties out three counters.) And in each container there are three counters. (Replaces the three counters.) How many counters would there be altogether?

J: (Looks ahead for seven seconds.) Eighteen!

A: Tell me how you worked that out.

J: (Points to each of the six containers in turn.) I said three, six, nine, twelve, fifteen, and then I just counted on – three.

A: Tell me the numbers that you used to count on. You got to fifteen, and then you said?

J: (After three seconds, while looking at Anna makes three pointing actions in co-ordination with counting.) Sixteen, seventeen, eighteen.

Discussion of Video Excerpt 3

Jenna used skip counting by threes up to fifteen to count five groups of three counters and then counted-on by ones to count the sixth group of three counters. Jenna's strategy is indicative of Level 3, that is, Figurative Composite Grouping, because she counted in multiples of three in order to count six groups of three, in the case where the individual items in each group are screened.

Level 4: Repeated Abstract Composite Grouping

The child at Level 4 has constructed a conceptual structure labelled an 'abstract composite unit' in which the child is simultaneously aware of both the composite and unitary aspects of three, for example. The child can use repeated addition to solve multiplication tasks and repeated subtraction to solve division tasks, and can do so in the absence of visible or screened items. On a multiplicative task involving six groups of three items, in which each group is separately screened, the child is aware of each group as an abstract composite unit. Construction of abstract composite units is associated with Stage 5 on SEAL (see Chapter 4). Thus in the case of children who have significant experience with multiplication and division situations as well as addition and subtraction situations, it is likely that being at Level 4 on early multiplication and division is contemporaneous with being at Stage 5 in terms of SEAL.

Video Excerpt 4: Emily and Jamal

E: If twelve cakes were shared among the children and they got four cakes each, how many children would there be?

J: (After two seconds.) Three!

E: How did you work that out?

J: Umm, I was trying to figure it out by fours.

E: Okay. So how did you figure it out by fours? What did you do?

J: One, two, three, four (slight pause), five, six, seven, eight (slight pause), nine, ten, eleven, twelve. (Looks at Emily.)

E: Hmm, hmm. (Looks at Jamal.)

J: (After two seconds.) By counting one, two, three, fours.

E: Hmm, hmm. And then what did you do after you went one, two, three, four?

J: I – , I tried to figure out what three fours equalled and it equalled twelve.

E: (Places out seven piggy banks and a large collection of counters.)

I want you to use exactly twenty counters to make piggy banks that have five counters in them. And tell me how many piggy banks you need?

J: (Immediately, while shrugging his shoulders, looking at Emily and smiling.) Four!

E: How did you do that?

J: I counted. (Points to four piggy banks in turn.) Like, that was one five, ten, fifteen, twenty.

Discussion of Video Excerpt 4

Jamal's solution of the first task was relatively sophisticated because when he counted by ones from one to twelve, he was double counting. His count from one to twelve was an object on which he could focus in order to determine how many times he made four counts. Presumably Jamal anticipated he could do this prior to commencing his count. Jamal's explanation 'By counting one, two, three, fours' is ambiguous because the number of groups (i.e. three) is one less than the number in each group (i.e. four). Thus Emily interpreted this explanation as a count from 'one' to 'four' whereas, for Jamal, 'fours' in his explanation referred to groups of four. His explanation referred to counting the groups of four rather than the items in one of the groups (e.g. the first group). Jamal solved the second task by counting by fives to twenty and keeping track of the number of counts. Emily provided seven piggy banks and a large collection of counters but Jamal did not use the counters in his solution. Inherent in each of Jamal's solutions is the construction of an abstract composite unit. On the first task Jamal simultaneously regards 'four' as four ones (i.e. in his count by ones from one to twelve) and one four (i.e. in his keeping track of the number of times he makes four counts). Similarly on the second task, the multiples of five ('five', 'ten', etc.) signify for Jamal both another five and five more ones. Jamal's strategies are indicative of Level 4, that is, Repeated Abstract Composite Grouping.

Level 5: Multiplication and Division as Operations

The child at Level 5 can co-ordinate two composite units in the context of multiplication or division. In a task such as six threes or six groups of three, for example, the child is aware of both six and three as abstract composite units whereas, at Level 4, the child is aware of three as an abstract composite unit but is not aware of six as an abstract composite unit. The child at Level 5 can immediately recall or quickly derive many of the basic facts of multiplication and division and may use multiplication facts to derive division facts. At Level 5, the commutative principle of multiplication (e.g. $5 \times 3 = 3 \times 5$) and the inverse relationship between multiplication and division are within the child's zone of proximal development. Thus, for example, the child might be aware that six threes is the same as three sixes and might use $4 \times 8 = 32$ to work out $32 \div 4$.

Video Excerpt 5: Richard and Aimee

R: There are twelve tables and four children are seated at each table. How many children are there?

A: Six times four is twenty-four so twelve times four is forty-eight.

R: Why did you use six times four?

A: I just doubled six times, so it's twelve times.

R: There are forty-two stickers to be shared fairly among seven children. How many stickers do they get each?

A: Three by seven is twenty-one, so forty-two divided by seven must be six.

R: Why did you use three by seven first?

A: Because three by seven is twenty-one so that's half-way. Twenty-one and twenty-one is forty-two. So it's double three.

Discussion of Video Excerpt 5

In solving the first task when Aimee said 'six times four is twenty-four so twelve times four is forty-eight', 'six' and 'twelve' as well as 'four' were abstract composite units for her. Aimee simultaneously regarded 'six fours' as standing for one unit, that is, one lot of 'six fours' (which could be doubled), and as 'six lots of four'. Aimee solutions were very sophisticated in relative terms because she used multiplication facts that she knew automatically (i.e. $6 \times 4 = 24$ and $3 \times 7 = 21$ respectively) to work out 12×4 and $42 \div 7$. Using an automatized multiplication fact to solve a different multiplicative task or to solve a divisional task are indicative of Level 5, that is, Multiplication and Division as Operations.

Assessment Schedule for Early Multiplication and Division

The Assessment Schedule for Early Multiplication and Division consists of six task groups. Task Group 1 involves number word sequences of multiples and Task Groups 2–6 involve multiplicative and divisional tasks. Across the Task Groups the tasks become progressively more difficult. Finally, the general guidelines and procedures for conducting assessment interviews presented in Chapter 6 apply equally well to the assessment tasks which appear below.

Task Group 1: Tasks Involving Forward Number Word Sequences of Multiples

(a) *Count by twos. I'll tell you when to stop.*   (Stop at 20.)
(b) *Count by tens. I'll tell you when to stop.*   (Stop at 120.)
(c) *Count by fives. I'll tell you when to stop.*   (Stop at 55.)
(d) *Count by threes. I'll tell you when to stop.*   (Stop at 15.)

Task Group 2: Tasks Involving Visible Items Arranged in Rows or Arrays

(a) Ask the child to look away while you place out ten rows of two counters.
Count these counters and tell me how many there are altogether.
(b) Similar to (a) using five rows of three counters.
(c) Display a 4 × 5 array of dots, that is, four rows and five columns. Indicate rows in turn. *How many rows are there?*
How many dots in each row?
How many dots altogether?
Turn the array through 90 degrees. *How many dots altogether now?*

Task Group 3: Tasks Involving Equal Groups of Visible Items

(a) Multiplication. Place out four plates with three counters on each plate. *How many plates are there? There are three counters on each plate, how many counters are there altogether?*
(b) Partitive sharing. Place out a pile of fifteen counters. *Here are fifteen counters. If we shared them equally among three children how many would each child get?*
(c) Quotitive sharing. Place out a pile of twelve counters. *Here are twelve counters. If we shared them equally among some children so they each got four how many children would there be?*
(d) Partitive sharing with redistribution. Place out a pile of twenty-four counters. *Here are twenty-four counters. If we shared them equally among three children how many would each child get?*
If I now shared them equally among four children how many would each get?

Task Group 4: Tasks Involving Screened Items

(a) Multiplication with equal groups.
Ask the child to look away while you place out four screens with

three counters under each screen. Momentarily display the counters under one screen. *Each screen has three counters under it. How many counters altogether?*

(b) Partition division with equal groups.
(Place out a pile of twelve counters and three piggy banks.) *Share these counters equally among the three banks and tell me how many counters there will be in each bank?* Ensure that the child is not able to count the counters after having shared them.

(c) Quotition division with equal groups.
(Place out a pile of thirty counters and seven piggy banks.) *Use twenty of the counters to make banks with five counters in each and tell me how many banks you will use.*

(d) Multiplication with an array.
Using a 5 × 3 array, use one screen to screen the upper two rows and a second screen to screen the lower three rows. Unscreen the upper two rows for a few seconds. *How many rows do you see? Rescreen the two rows. There are three more rows under this screen. How many counters altogether?*

(e) Quotition division with an array.
Using a 6 × 2 array, screen five rows and leave the uppermost row unscreened. *How many dots in this row? There are twelve dots altogether. How many rows altogether?*

Task Group 5: Tasks Presented without Visible or Screened Items

(a) Multiplication. *Six children have 5 marbles each. How many marbles altogether?*

(b) Quotition division. *There are twelve bananas and each child is given two bananas each. How many children are there altogether?*

(c) Partition division. *If we shared eighteen apples among three children, how many apples would each child get?*

(d) Quotition division with remainder. *There are seventeen flowers and each person is given five flowers. How many people are there and how many flowers are left over?*

(e) Partition division with remainder. *If we shared fourteen cookies equally among four children, how many cookies would each child get and how many would be left over?*

Task Group 6: Commutativity and Inverse Relationship

(a) *What does this say?* 9 × 7
How would you work this out?
Can you tell me another way to work it out?

(b) *What does this say?* 3 × 7
     What does this say? 7 × 3
     What can you tell me about these two problems?
(c) *What is the answer to this problem?* 8 × 4
     Can you use that to help you do this problem? 32 ÷ 4?
(d) *If I tell you that eight times seven is fifty-six* (show 8 × 7 = 56)
     can you use these numbers and signs to make a division? 8, 7,
     56, =, ÷

Materials Required: Early Multiplication and Division Assessment
Arrays: 4 × 5; 5 × 3; 6 × 2.
Counters: thirty of one colour.
Screens: two larger size pieces of cardboard (e.g. 20 cm × 30 cm).
Screens: four smaller size pieces of cardboard (e.g. 8 cm × 12 cm).
Paper plates: four.
Piggy-banks: seven.
Problems written on cards: 9 × 7; 3 × 7; 7 × 3; 8 × 4; 32 ÷ 4; 8 × 7
     = 56.
Numbers and signs on cards: 8, 7, 56, =, ÷.

Summary Guidelines for Determining Level of Early Multiplication and Division Knowledge

These guidelines should be considered in conjunction with the descriptions and illustrations of each of the levels (as presented earlier in this chapter), and with the scenarios and their explanations (as presented later in this chapter).

Level 1. Level 1 is characterized by perceptual counting by ones. A child is assessed at Level 1 if they are able to solve tasks such as those in Task Groups 2 and 3 and, in doing so, count by ones rather than count in multiples.
Level 2. Level 2 is characterized by the use of multiplicative counting strategies in cases where items are visible. A child is assessed at Level 2 if they are able to solve tasks such as those in Task Groups 2 and 3, and count in multiples when so doing.
Level 3. A child at Level 3 can construct numerical composites but not abstract composite units. Level 3 is characterized by the use of multiplicative counting strategies in cases where items are screened. A child is assessed at Level 3 if they are able to solve tasks such as Tasks (a), (b), (c) and (d) in Task Group 4, and

count in multiples, or use addition or subtraction when so doing.

Level 4. A child at Level 4 can construct abstract composite units but not composite units of composite units. A child is assessed at Level 4 if they are able to solve tasks such as Task (e) in Task Group 4 and the tasks in Task Group 5, and count in multiples, or use addition or subtraction when so doing.

Level 5. A child at Level 5 can construct abstract composite units, the elements of which are also abstract composite units (i.e. composites of composites). A child is assessed at Level 5 if they are able to solve tasks such as those in Task Group 5 using known or quickly derived facts, or if they solve Tasks (a), (b) (c) or (d) in Task Group 6.

Can You Identify the Child's Level of Early Multiplication and Division Knowledge?

This section is similar to Chapter 5 where the reader was challenged to apply the SEAL model to classify children on the basis of strategies used to solved numerical tasks. In this section five scenarios describing children's solutions of multiplicative and divisional tasks are presented. Each of the five levels of early multiplication and division knowledge is exemplified by one scenario. The task for the reader is to identify the most appropriate level for each scenario.

Solutions and explanations follow each scenario and identify the particular level for each. Included among the discussions are some important general points about children's early numerical strategies.

Scenario 1: Charlotte and Anthony
In this scenario Anthony's first two tasks are to establish the numerosities of a screened 5 × 3 array and a partially screened 5 × 4 array. Following this Anthony is presented with a divisional task involving quotitive sharing.

C: (Places out a 5 × 3 array with one screen covering three rows and a second screen covering the other two rows. Briefly unscreens and then rescreens the three rows.) Under here there are three rows of three and under here there are two rows of three. How many rows are there altogether?

A: Five.

C: How many dots in each row?

A: Three.

C: How many dots are there altogether?

A: (After six seconds.) Fifteen!

C: How did you work that out?

A: I said, three, six, nine, and three more makes twelve and three more makes fifteen.

C: (Places out a 5 × 4 array on which twelve dots in a 4 × 3 array are screened.) I've covered part of this dot pattern. How many dots are there altogether?

A: (Looks at the array and moves his head from left to right and back five times in co-ordination with five subvocal counts.) There is – twelve!

C: How did you work that out?

A: I counted all the rows.

C: Tell me how you counted them.

A: (Points to each row of four in turn.) I went four, eight, twelve, umm – , sixteen, twenty!

C: There are twelve biscuits and the children are given two biscuits each. How many children would there be?

A: (Places his right hand on the desk and speaks softly.) Twelve biscuits – . (After 11 seconds.) There is – .

C: Pardon?

A: There is twelve biscuits (pauses) and we gotta share 'em.

C: Hmm, hmm. So that they get two biscuits each. How many children would there be?

A: (Looks ahead and then quickly moves his right hand twice along the desk.) One, two (subvocally. As before, quickly moves his hand twice), three, four (subvocally, and then moves his hand twice for a third time) five, six – (subvocally. Pauses for two seconds, and then makes four pairs of two movements on the desk in co-ordination with counting subvocally.) One, two – ; three, four – ; five, six; seven, eight – . (Pauses for one second, and then makes three pairs of two movements on the desk in co-ordination with counting subvocally.) One, two – ; three, four – ; five, six – . (Pauses briefly, and then taps the desk five times in a 2-2-1 pattern in co-ordination with counting subvocally.) One, two – ; three, four – ; five – . (Touches the desk three times.) Three children.

Scenario 1: Charlotte and Anthony – Level 3

Anthony used skip counting and repeated addition to establish the numerosity of a screened 5 × 3 array and a partially screened 5 × 4 array. In explaining his solution of the task involving the 5 × 3 array he said 'three, six, nine, and three more makes twelve, and three more makes fifteen'. He similarly explained his solution of the task involving a 5 × 4 array. These solutions indicate that Anthony is at least at Level 3 because he solved tasks in which the items where not visible and in doing so counted equal groups by multiples. That the task involving quotitive sharing did not involve visible or screened items is significant in determining Anthony's level. Anthony did not use repeated subtraction or repeated addition when attempting to solve this task. Having done so would indicate that he could conceptualize 'two' as an abstract composite unit. He could regard 'two' simultaneously as two ones and one two. By way of contrast Anthony attempted to enact making groups of two using twelve imaginary biscuits. But he was unable to keep track of the number of groups and the number of biscuits remaining after he had enacted making three groups of two. In the absence of visible or screened items it was necessary for Anthony to attempt to enact making equal groups of two from twelve. Because 'two' was not an abstract composite unit for Anthony and because he could count in multiples to solve tasks involving equal groups, he is judged to be at Level 3, that is, Figurative Composite Grouping.

Scenario 2: Amanda and Joshua

In this scenario Joshua's first task is to produce the number word sequence of multiples of three, his second task is to establish the numerosity of a 5 × 3 array, and his third is to establish the numerosity of a 5 × 4 array. On the fourth task he is asked to count the 5 × 4 array by counting the rows of five rather than the rows of four.

A: Count by threes.
J: Three, six, (after four seconds) nine, (after three seconds) twelve, (after two seconds) fifteen, (after four seconds) fifteen.
A: Okay stop. Thank you. (Places out five rows of three counters arranged in a 5 × 3 array.) Can you count those now?
J: (Places a finger on each counter in the first row and moves the counters.) Three, (similarly moves the second row) six, (moves the next three rows in co-ordination with saying the number words) nine, twelve, fifteen.
A: (Places out a 5 × 4 array of dots.) How many dots are there altogether?
J: Four, and four makes eight, nine, ten, eleven, twelve, thirteen.
A: Can you count the rows in fives the other way (indicates appropriately)?
J: (Places hand on row of five.) That's five, ten, fifteen, (pauses briefly) sixteen, seventeen, eighteen, nineteen, twenty.

Scenario 2: Amanda and Joshua – Level 2

Joshua counted a 5 × 3 array of counters by moving each row of three in co-ordination with saying the multiples of three. After unsuccessfully attempting to count a 5 × 4 array by fours he counted the array by fives to fifteen and continued by ones to count the fourth row of five. Because he could use multiples of three or five to count visible collections, Joshua is judged to be at Level 2, that is, Perceptual Counting in Multiples. Joshua's strategies differ from Anthony's (Scenario 1) because they involved counting visible collections by multiples, whereas Anthony's strategies involved counting screened collections by multiples.

Scenario 3 – Steven and Aaron

In this scenario Aaron is presented with two tasks, each of which involves establishing the numerosity of an array (5 × 3 and 5 × 4). Following this he is presented with a divisional task involving quotitive sharing and a multiplicative task.

S: (Places out a 5 × 3 array with one screen covering three rows and a second screen covering the other two rows. Briefly unscreens and then rescreens the three rows.) Under here there are three rows of three and under here there are two rows of three. How many dots are there altogether?

A: (After five seconds.) Fifteen!

S: How did you work that out?

A: Because you said there were three rows down the bottom and there's two rows at the top. And that makes five. And you do five times three.

S: (Places out a 5 × 4 array on which twelve dots in a 4 × 3 array are screened.) Now this time, we've covered part of that pattern of dots. Can you tell me how many dots on that whole page?

A: (Looks at the array and counts subvocally.) One, two, three, four; one, two, three, four, five. (Looks up and answers after one second.) Twenty!

S: How did you know that?

A: Because I counted four up top and five along the side.

S: And how did that help?

A: Umm – , well you're – , five times four equals twenty.

S: Twelve cakes were shared among some children so that they got four each. How many children were there.

A: (After two seconds.) Three!

S: How did you get that answer?
A: Because four times three equals twelve.
S: Six children have five marbles each. How many marbles altogether?
A: (Immediately.) Six fives are thirty. Thirty.
S: Can you tell me how you got thirty?
A: I just timesed six by five. Six fives are thirty.

Scenario 3: Steven and Aaron – Level 5

Aaron used automatized multiplication facts to solve two multiplicative tasks. The first of these involved a screened 5 × 3 array and the second involved a partially screened 5 × 4 array. Aaron also used automatized multiplication facts to solve a divisional and a multiplicative task. These tasks did not involve visible or screened items. In the case of the two tasks involving arrays, Aaron's strategies can be contrasted with Anthony's because Anthony counted in multiples whereas Aaron used automatized facts. Because of his prevalent use of automatized facts to solve tasks, Aaron is judged to be at Level 5, that is, Known Multiplication and Division Facts.

Scenario 4: Jeremy and Chantelle

In the this scenario Chantelle's first task is to produce the number word sequence of multiples of three and her second task is to establish the numerosity of a 5 × 3 array of counters.

J: Can you count by threes for me? I'll tell you when to stop.
C: (Immediately.) Three – . (Looks ahead. After four seconds.) Seven. (Looks at Jeremy, smiles and shakes her head.)
J: Would you like to start again?
C: (Immediately.) Three, six, (after three seconds) twelve.
J: (After six seconds.) You can stop there.
J: I'm going to put out some counters now. (Places out five rows of three counters arranged in a 5 × 3 array.) They're arranged in threes aren't they? Could you show me how you'd count those counters by threes? You can move them if you would like to.
C: (Counts subvocally from one to three in co-ordination with pointing to each counter in the first row in turn. Places a finger on each counter in the first row and moves them a small distance.) Three. (Counts subvocally from four to six in co-ordination with pointing to each counter in the second row in turn. Then moves the second row a small distance.) Six. (Similarly counts the counters in the third row subvocally and then moves them). Nine. (Similarly with the fourth and fifth rows.) Twelve, fifteen.

Scenario 4: Jeremy and Chantelle – Level 1

Chantelle was not able to produce the number word sequence of multiples of three. In the task which involved establishing the numerosity of a 5 × 3 array of counters she appeared to produce the number word sequence of multiples of three up to fifteen in co-ordination with moving successive rows of three counters. Nevertheless, in doing this she subvocally counted each row by ones prior to uttering the appropriate multiple of three, for example she said 'seven, eight, nine' subvocally and then said aloud, 'nine'. This counting did not constitute counting by threes. Her inability to produce the number word sequence of multiples of threes on the first task provides a further indication that she could not count in multiples. Thus Chantelle is judged to be at Level 1, that is, Initial Grouping. Chantelle's strategies differ from Joshua's (Scenario 2) because they involve counting visible collections of equal groups by ones rather than counting by multiples as was the case with Joshua's strategies.

Scenario 5: Meghan and Orana

In this scenario Orana's first task is to establish the numerosity of a screened 5 × 3 array. Her second task is to establish the numerosity of the screened 5 × 3 array after Meghan has turned it through 90 degrees (approximately). Her third task is a multiplicative task (4 × 3), her fourth is a divisional task involving quotitive sharing, and her fifth is a divisional task involving partitive sharing.

M: (Briefly displays and then screens a 5 × 3 array of dots.) How many dots are there in each row?

O: Five.

M: (Displays the array and points to a row of three dots.) This is a row here.

O: Oh. Three!

M: Three in each row. How many rows are there?

O: (After three seconds.) Five!

M: (Screens the array.) How many dots are there altogether?

O: (Looks at the screen and counts subvocally. After six seconds.) Fifteen!

M: How did you know that?

O: Because three and three makes six (waves her hand over the first two rows of the array), and another three makes (pauses for two seconds) nine, and another three makes umm twelve, and then another three makes fifteen!

M: Thank you! (Unscreens the array and rotates it through 90 degrees.) If I was to turn them around that way how many dots now?

O: (Immediately.) Umm, fifteen!

M: How did you know that?

O: Because when you turn it around there was fifteen and then when you turn it this way there's fifteen.

M: Four children have three pencils each. How many pencils altogether?

O: (After 3 seconds.) Twelve!

M: How did you work that out?

O: I was counting by – (pauses briefly) threes?

M: Hmm, hmm.

O: And it made twelve.

M: Orana there are twelve biscuits and children were given two biscuits each. How many children would there be?

O: Umm, two – , two, four, six, eight, ten, twelve. Six.

M: How did you know that?

O: Because two plus two plus two plus two plus two plus two equals six.

M: Good thinking. If we shared eighteen lollies among three children, how many would each child get?

O: (Looks to her left. After five seconds.) Six!

M: And what did you do to work that one out?

O: I was counting by sixes first.

Scenario 5: Meghan and Orana – Level 4

Orana used repeated addition of three in explaining how she counted a 5 × 3 array. In similar vein, she said 'I was counting by – threes' to explain how she solved a multiplicative task involving three groups of four pencils and she counted by twos to twelve to solve a division task involving quotitive sharing. Her solution to the partitive sharing task (18 shared among 3) was relatively sophisticated because it seemed to involve using six as an estimation. Knowing that the 5 × 3 array contained the same number of dots after it was rotated as before (i.e. 15) indicates she could conserve quantity rather than that she had a generalized knowledge of the commutative principle of multiplication. For these reasons Orana is judged to be at Level 4, that is, Repeated Abstract Composite Grouping. Her solution of the task involving a 5 × 3 array can be contrasted with Aaron's (Scenario 3) because Aaron used an automatized fact (5 × 3 = 15), whereas Orana used repeated addition of three. Anthony (Scenario 1) solved this task using a strategy similar to that used by Orana, that is, by counting in multiples of three to nine and then adding three twice to obtain fifteen. One can conclude that a task involving counting how many counters in all, in an array, that is, a multiplicative array task, is unlikely to discriminate between children at Level 3 and those at Level 4, whereas a divisional array task, that is, where the number of items in all and the number of items in each row is specified, might serve this purpose. Finally, Orana's solution of the divisional task involving quotitive sharing – 'there are twelve biscuits and the children are given two each, etc.' – can be contrasted with Anthony's (Scenario 1). In this task Orana counted by twos whereas Anthony attempted to enact arranging twelve into groups of two. Orana could regard 'two' as a unit (i.e. one 'two'), that is, as an abstract composite unit that could be counted. For Anthony 'two' was a numerical composite (i.e. two 'ones') that resulted when he enacted making successive groups of two.

Exemplary Instructional Tasks for Early Multiplication and Division

This section provides detailed descriptions of exemplary instructional tasks that have particular relevance for early multiplication and division. Some of the tasks that appear below are similar to tasks in the assessment schedule that appears in this chapter. The purpose of this section is to provide a comprehensive and detailed listing of basic instructional tasks in early multiplication and division. All the tasks listed below can be used in formal and informal assessment, and can be adapted in various ways for individualized or class instruction.

These tasks may be used to develop advanced counting strategies and composite grouping, initially in settings where items are visible and then in settings where they are screened. These settings include equal groups of discrete items and arrays. Both are considered important for the development of multiplication and division knowledge. Finally, both quotitive and partitive grouping are included in the divisional tasks.

1   Tasks Involving Number Word Sequences of Multiples

1.1 *Forward Number Word Sequences of Multiples Commencing from the First Multiple*

Ask the child to count by twos. Do not tell the child in advance where to stop. Similarly, ask the child to count by threes, by fives and by tens. More advanced children may be asked to count by fours, etc. Of interest is how facile the child is in saying the number word sequence and where the child stops.

1.2 Forward Number Word Sequences of Multiples Commencing from a Higher Multiple

Ask the child to start at six (fourteen, etc.) and count by twos. Similarly, ask the child to start at twelve (twenty-four, etc.) and count by threes, to start at thirty-five and count by fives, etc.

1.3 Backward Number Word Sequences of Multiples

Ask the child to count backwards by twos, starting at ten. Similarly, ask the child to count backwards from thirty by fives and from eighteen by threes.

2 Tasks Involving Equal Groups

Grouping and Counting Visible, Partially Screened and Screened Groups

The term 'counting' is used here in the sense of 'establishing the numerosity of'. It is not intended that the child should necessarily count by ones nor is it intended that the child should necessarily count by multiples. Thus, in these tasks instead of saying 'count the dots', one might say, 'Can you figure out how many dots there are here?' Posing the task in this way is likely to provide more licence to the child in terms of the strategy used to solve the task.

2.1 Making Equal Groups

Place out a pile of approximately twenty counters (all of one colour). Ask the child to make four groups of two. Similarly, ask the child to make six groups of three, three groups of four, etc.

2.2 Describing Visible Groups

Display five groups of two counters. Rather than placing out the counters by ones or twos in full view of the child, ask the child to look away while you are placing out the counters. Ask the child to describe what they see. Similarly, six groups of three counters and three groups of five counters each arranged in a domino-five pattern. Of interest is the extent to which the child refers to groups, the number of groups, equal groups and the number in each group or the total.

2.3 Counting Visible Groups

Each of the tasks in 2.2 can be used as a counting task. Note the child's strategy, for example counting by ones or by twos. If the child counts by ones, ask if they have another way to figure out how many dots in the groups altogether.

2.4 Describing Screened Groups

As in 2.2 above, ask the child to look away and then place out three groups of two counters. Ask the child to look back and then briefly display the equal groups. Ask the child to describe what they saw. Similarly with four groups of four counters and five groups of three counters. Of interest is the extent to which the child can describe the groups and the way in which the child describes them.

2.5 Counting Screened Groups

Each of the tasks in 2.4 can be used as a counting task. As in 2.3 above, note the child's strategy.

2.6 Partitive Division using a Screened Collection

Briefly display and then screen a collection of twelve counters. Ask the child to figure out how many counters would be in each of three equal groups.

2.7 Quotitive Division using a Screened Collection

Briefly display and then screen a collection of twenty counters. Ask the child to figure out how many groups of five counters could be made from twenty counters.

3   Tasks Involving Arrays

These tasks involve using rectangular arrays of dots or counters. For each of the tasks in 2.1 to 2.5 above there is a corresponding task involving an array rather than equal groups. The label '5 × 2', for example, indicates an array with five rows and two columns.

3.1 Making an Array

Place out a pile of approximately twenty counters (all of one colour). Ask the child to make three rows of four, etc.

3.2 Describing a Visible Array

Display an array of dots (e.g. 5 × 2) and ask the child to describe what they see.

3.3 Counting a Visible Array

Ask the child to figure out how many dots in the array (e.g. 5 × 2). If the child counts by ones, ask if they have another way to figure out how many dots in the array.

3.4 Describing a Screened Array

Briefly display and then screen an array (e.g. 2 × 4). Ask the child to describe what they saw.

3.5 Counting a Screened Array
Briefly display and then screen an array. Ask the child to figure out how many dots in the array.

3.6 Rotating an Array
(This task can be used as an extension to any of the above tasks where the child has counted the dots in an array.) Rotate the array through 90 degrees and ask the child how many dots there are now.

3.7 Quotitive Division
Using a 5 × 3 array, screen four of the rows leaving the uppermost row unscreened. Ask the child how many dots in the unscreened row. Tell the child there are five rows in all and ask them to figure out how many dots altogether.

Summary

This chapter has focused on an extension of the Learning Framework in Number to the area of multiplication and division. An overview of the development of early multiplication and division knowledge and an associated model consisting of five levels are presented. Illustrations of children solving problems are used to exemplify the levels and an assessment schedule for early multiplication and division knowledge is set out. The chapter also includes five scenarios for which the reader is challenged to determine an appropriate level, and solutions and explanations of the scenarios. The chapter concludes with a list of exemplary tasks for instruction in early multiplication and division.

Appendix 1

Reporting Outcomes from Mathematics Recovery and Count Me In Too

This appendix reports outcomes of two implementations of the Mathematics Recovery Programme – in Australia, in 1994, and in the USA, in 1995–96 – and outcomes of an evaluation of the Count Me In Too project in Australia, in 1996. The reports relating to MR focus on the progress of participating children and illustrate the levels of student progress that can be expected in an implementation of MR. These reports also demonstrate how the Learning Framework in Number is used to document progress of relatively large numbers of children over an extended period (e.g. over the period of a school year). The report relating to CMIT focuses on the perceptions of participating teachers and other adult personnel associated with the programme, and the progress of a sample of 37 of the participating children over the course of a 15-week instructional period.

Children's Progress in Mathematics Recovery

Since 1992, the Mathematics Recovery Programme has been implemented in groups of schools in Australia, the USA and the UK. In each implementation the progress of participating children was assessed and documented, using the Mathematics Recovery assessment. For each participant, the assessment results are recorded in and maintained via a database. In this database, the record for each child includes the stage and levels at the time of the pre- and post-assessments, as well as particulars such as name, date of birth, class teacher, MR teacher, school, number of teaching sessions, length of teaching cycle in weeks, and dates of the pre- and post-assessments. The database constitutes the source for summary reports on the progress of participants. By way of example, the following section focuses on the progress of participants in the 1994 Australian cohort and the 1995–96 USA cohort. In all cases the children are Year 1, that is, in their second year of school, and are typically six or seven years of age.

Using the Learning Framework in Number (LFIN) to Document Children's Progress.

The Learning Framework in Number is described in detail in Chapter 2. LFIN consists of ten aspects of children's early numerical knowledge. In the following two reports of children's progress in Mathematics Recovery, SEAL – the primary aspect of LFIN – and three other aspects – FNWS, BNWS and Numeral Identification – are used to document progress of participants in Mathematics Recovery. This involves applications of the models that are set out in tabular form in Chapter 2 (see Tables 2.2, 2.4, 2.5 and 2.6).

The 1994 Australian Cohort

In the Australian implementation in 1994, there were 12 participating teachers in 11 schools, and in each school the project operated for approximately 30 weeks, that is, from midway through first term (March) until midway through fourth term (November). Typically, the teachers worked on the project in the morning half of each day. In the initial two or three weeks of the 30-week period and also the final two or three weeks, the teachers completed interview-based assessments with participating children and counterparts.

Eight of the teachers had completed an MR professional development course in 1992 or 1993. These teachers commenced MR teaching cycles after the initial two- or three-week assessment period. The other four teachers commenced MR teaching cycles after six weeks. This enabled them to undertake the first phase of the MR professional development programme prior to commencing teaching cycles. After the initial six weeks all 12 teachers attended ongoing professional development meetings held once every two weeks. Eleven of the teachers individually taught four children, for 30 minutes daily, for four days per week. The other teacher individually taught two children per day, for four days per week.

The Participating Children

There were 89 participating children in all. Of these, 14 had fewer than 25 teaching sessions. This report focuses on the remaining 75 participants – eight in each of four schools, seven in each of two schools, six in each of four, and five in one. Their teaching cycles ranged in length from 7 to 20 weeks, with an average of 13 weeks. Their number of teaching sessions ranged from 25 to 69, and was on average 41.

Summary of Participants' Progress

Table A1.1 shows the numbers of participants at given stages in terms of SEAL, on the pre- and post-assessments. For example, of five children initially at Stage 0, three progressed to Stage 1 and two progressed to Stage 3. Of 26 children initially at Stage 1, two remained at Stage 1, four progressed to Stage 2, 12 progressed to Stage 3, five to Stage 4 and three to Stage 5. Of the 75 participants, 72 (i.e. 96 per cent) were at Stage 2 or lower at the time of pre-assessment, and at the time of post-assessment 63 (i.e. 84 per cent) were at Stage 3 or above. Fifty-eight (i.e. 77 per cent) of the participants were initially at Stage 1 or 2 and finally at Stage 3, 4, or 5. This typifies the progress made

Table A1.1 1994 Australian cohort: numbers and percentages of participants at given stages on pre- and post-assessments

Pre						
	1	*2*	*3*	*4*	*5*	*Total*
0	3 (60%)	0	2 (40%)	0	0	5 (100%)
1	2 (8%)	4 (15%)	12 (46%)	5 (19%)	3 (12%)	26 (100%)
2	0	3 (7%)	29 (71%)	7 (17%)	2 (5%)	41 (100%)
3	0	0	2 (67%)	1 (33%)	0	3 (100%)
Total	5	7	45	13	5	75

Numbers of Children at Given Stages spanning header; *Post* spanning columns 1–5.

by these participants and can be reasonably regarded as significant progress.

Progress of Lowest Attaining on Pre-Assessment

Table A1.2 shows the stage and levels on the pre- and post-assessments of five participants who can be regarded as the lowest attaining at the time of their pre-assessment. These were the only children who were at Stage 0 on the pre-assessment. The progress of the child listed first in Table A1.2, for example, can be summarized as follows. Initially he could not count the items of a visible collection, could not say the FNWS from 'one' to 'ten', and could not identify some or all of the numerals from '1' to '10'. At the conclusion of his teaching cycle he could count-on to solve addition problems, was facile with FNWSs in the range 'one' to 'thirty' and BNWSs in the range 'one' to 'ten', and could identify one- and two-digit numerals. In summary, he made substantial gains across all four aspects of early number knowledge.

Table A1.2 1994 Australian cohort: progress of the five children who were lowest attaining in the pre-assessment

	Boy /Girl	No. of teaching sessions	Stage in terms of SEAL		FNWS 0–5		BNWS 0–5		Numeral Identific'n 0–4	
1	B	65	0	3	0	4	0	3	0	3
2	G	57	0	1	1	3	0	3	0	1
3	B	42	0	1	1	3	0	0	0	1
4	B	61	0	1	3	3	0	3	1	3
5	B	44	0	3	3	5	3	4	1	4

Table A1.3 shows the stages or levels on each of the four models resulting from pre- and post-assessments of five participants who can be regarded as the highest attaining at the time of their post-assessment. The children listed second and third in Table A1.3, for example, made profound advancements over the course of 35 teaching sessions. They progressed from being percep-

Table A1.3 1994 Australian cohort: progress of the five children who were highest attaining in the post-assessment

	Boy /Girl	No. of teaching sessions	Stage in terms of SEAL		FNWS 0–5		BNWS 0–5		Numeral Identific'n 0–4	
1	G	46	1	5	3	5	2	5	2	4
2	B	35	1	5	3	5	3	5	1	4
3	B	35	1	5	3	5	3	5	1	4
4	B	35	2	5	3	5	1	5	1	3
5	G	49	2	5	3	5	3	5	2	3

tual counters, facile with FNWSs and BNWSs in the range 'one' to 'ten' only, and able to identify numerals to '10' only, to using strategies other than counting by ones when adding and subtracting, being facile with FNWSs and BNWSs to 'one hundred' and being able to identify numerals to '999'.

Progress of Participants Who Did Not Advance at Least One Stage
The children listed in Table A1.4 may be regarded as the seven children who,

Table A1.4: 1994 Australian cohort: progress of the seven children who did not advance by at least one stage

	Boy /Girl	No. of teaching sessions	Stage in terms of SEAL		FNWS 0–5		BNWS 0–5		Numeral Identific'n 0–4	
1	G	59	1	1	1	3	0	0	0	2
2	B	39	1	1	3	3	0	3	1	3
3	B	34	2	2	1	5	1	3	1	3
4	B	28	2	2	3	3	2	3	1	2
5	G	29	2	2	4	4	3	4	3	3
6	G	32	3	3	3	5	3	5	3	4
7	G	25	3	3	5	5	5	5	3	3

Table A1.5: 1994 Australian cohort: progress of the eight children in one school

	Boy /Girl	No. of teaching sessions	Stage in terms of SEAL		FNWS 0–5		BNWS 0–5		Numeral Identific'n 0–4	
1	B	46	1	3	3	4	2	4	1	3
2	G	46	1	5	3	5	2	5	2	4
3	B	35	1	5	3	5	3	5	1	4
4	B	37	2	3	2	5	3	3	1	3
5	G	35	2	5	3	5	3	5	2	3
6	G	31	2	3	4	5	3	4	1	4
7	G	39	2	3	4	5	3	5	1	4
8	G	26	2	3	5	5	1	5	1	4

in terms of the models, showed least progress because they did not advance by at least one stage. As can be seen in Table A1.4, all but the last listed of these children made advancements on at least one of the models.

Progress of Participants in One School
Table A1.5 has been included to exemplify progress of all of the participants of one school. As can be seen, all eight children progressed to at least Stage 3, and all made substantial gains in facility with number words and numeral identification.

The 1995–96 USA Cohort
In the 1995–96 school year, the USA implementation of MR operated with 15 teachers and 91 participants in 13 elementary schools, across two states in the south-east region of the USA. Pupil achievement in this implementation was reported by Wright *et al.* (1998). In each school, the project operated for approximately 18 weeks during each half of the school year. In the initial four weeks of each 18-week period and in the final two or three weeks, project teachers completed pre- and post-assessments of the participants. After the initial four weeks, participants were instructed individually for 30 minutes daily, for up to four days per week, for teaching cycles of duration from eight to twelve weeks. Project teachers undertook the first phase of the MR professional development program during the initial four weeks. After the initial four weeks these teachers attended ongoing professional development meetings held once every two weeks.

Summary of Participants' Progress
Table A1.6 shows the numbers of participants for this cohort at given stages in terms of SEAL, on the pre- and post-assessments. For example, of four children initially at Stage 0, one progressed to Stage 1 and three progressed to Stage 3. Of 63 children initially at Stage 1, three remained at Stage 1, ten progressed to Stage 2, 34 progressed to Stage 3, and 16 to Stage 4. Of the

Table A1.6 1995–96 USA cohort: numbers and percentages of participants at given stages on pre- and post-assessments

Pre	Numbers of Children at Given Stages					
	Post					
	1	2	3	4	5	Total
0	1 (25%)	0	3 (75%)	0	0	4 (100%)
1	3 (5%)	10 (16%)	34 (54%)	16 (25%)	0	63 (100%)
2	0	2 (9%)	10 (43%)	10 (43%)	1 (5%)	23 (100%)
3	0	0	1 (100%)	0	0	1 (100%)
Total	4	12	48	26	1	91

91 participants, 90 (i.e. 99 per cent) were at Stage 2 or lower at the time of pre-assessment, and at the time of post-assessment 75 (i.e. 82 per cent) were at Stage 3 or above. Seventy-one (i.e. 78 per cent) of the participants were initially at Stage 1 or 2 and finally at Stage 3, 4, or 5.

Progress across the two cohorts

The summary percentages given at the end of the previous paragraph, that is, 99 per cent, 82 per cent and 78 per cent, are very close in values to the corresponding percentages for the 1994 Australian cohort discussed earlier in this chapter, that is, 96 per cent, 84 per cent and 77 per cent respectively. Thus, in broad terms, the results for these two cohorts correspond closely. Similar results have been achieved for other cohorts, for example the 1992 and 1993 cohorts in Australia (Wright *et al.*, 1994; Wright *et al.*, 1996) and the 1996–97 cohort in the UK. The consistent pattern across all of the implementations of MR is that a large majority (i.e. at least 75 per cent) make very significant progress. They are initially at Stage 0, 1 or 2 and progress to at least Stage 3 in terms of SEAL and similarly make significant progress on the other three aspects of early number knowledge (i.e. FNWS, BNWS and Numeral Identification).

Evaluation of the Count Me In Too Project

The Count Me In Too project was discussed briefly in the Introduction. Count Me In Too is an innovative project in early mathematics which is being undertaken in the government school system in the Australian state of New South Wales. Count Me In Too can be regarded as an application of the theory and methods of MR to classroom teaching and to average and high-attaining children as well as to low-attaining children. As explained in the Introduction, as well as using LFIN as its central organizing framework, CMIT incorporates adaptations of MR's approaches to child assessment, teaching and teacher professional development. Count Me In Too has the goal of improving children's learning in early numeracy through teacher professional development. Count Me In Too is a school-based project and in each participating school, a district-based mathematics consultant (i.e. a district co-ordinator or supervisor in mathematics) works with a group of K–2 teachers to implement LFIN in their assessment and teaching of number. This involves the consultant meeting regularly with teachers and helping teachers to learn the distinctive assessment procedures and to understand the framework and its application to teaching.

Bobis (1996) conducted an independent evaluation of CMIT in its pilot year – 1996. In that year CMIT was implemented in a total of 13 schools across four of the state's 40 educational districts. Included among the participating schools were schools from large urban areas, from small regional cities and from rural areas. The project operated during the second and third terms (i.e. quarters) of the school year. Bobis's evaluation documents the perceptions of participating teachers, executive teachers (i.e. school principals and deputy or assistant principals) and district consultants about the program's effectiveness. The evaluation includes case studies of three of the participating teachers and five of the participating children.

Findings of the evaluation included:

1. Most teachers were considered [by consultants] to have gained a great deal, both professionally and personally, from the project (Bobis, 1996, p. 10).
2. Consultants gained a great deal of intrinsic satisfaction from the observable positive outcomes of the children and teachers (*ibid.*).
3. [Consultants] considered that teachers had become more reflective about their practice, had changed their classroom practice and had developed a deeper understanding of how children learn mathematics (*ibid.*).
4. All teachers considered that they had gained knowledge relating to content, strategies [or] how children learn mathematics (*ibid.*, p. 20).
5. Executive staff considered teachers involved in the project to have benefited both professionally and personally (*ibid.*).
6. All teachers and executive staff members considered that the project had positive cognitive and/or attitudinal outcomes for the children . . . (*ibid.*).
7. Generally teachers and executive staff members were positive about the overall outcomes of the project . . . (*ibid.*).
8. All case study teachers indicated that they had changed their classroom practice as a result of [the project]. They asked more challenging questions of their children and allowed them more opportunities to explore, discuss and reflect on their mathematics. Two [of the three case study teachers] considered the impact of the project would influence their teaching for the rest of their careers (*ibid.*, p. 30).
9. All [three] case study teachers considered that they had developed professionally. They considered their content knowledge of mathematics to have improved and their understanding of how children learn mathematics to have increased (*ibid.*).
10. Two [of the three case study teachers] indicated that children were more aware of their thinking strategies for solving problems and were able to clearly explain how they solved computations (*ibid.*, p. 31).

The evaluation also reports on the progress of a sample of 37 of the participating children in terms of the models of the LFIN, as indicated by pre- and post-assessments relating to an instructional period of approximately 15 weeks. It was found that:

1. Approximately three-quarters of children in the sample were using more sophisticated strategies to solve simple addition and subtraction problems at the end of the instructional period than they were at the start of the project (Bobis, p. 38).
2. Approximately 90 per cent of children in the sample progressed at least

one stage on two or more aspects of numerical development (*ibid.*).
3. Children determined to be initially the most advanced made the greatest progress, while children of lower ability progressed at a slower rate (*ibid.*).
4. Many children not only used sophisticated strategies to solve computational problems, but were able to justify their responses by clearly explaining their thinking (*ibid.*).

The evaluation of CMIT in its pilot year of 1996 can be regarded as a solid endorsement of LFIN and the approaches to assessment and teaching used in CMIT and MR. Participation in the project resulted in important benefits both for teachers and for children. Teachers' knowledge of mathematics content increased as did their understanding of children's numerical strategies and how children learn mathematics. The participating children developed more advanced mathematical knowledge and more sophisticated numerical strategies, and were better able to justify their solutions. Since 1996, CMIT has been implemented in hundreds of schools across all 40 educational districts of New South Wales. This wide-scale implementation has been facilitated by district-based (i.e. one per district) K–8 numeracy consultants (i.e. co-ordinators or supervisors in mathematics), who have participated in statewide professional development meetings focusing on the program.

In each school in which CMIT is implemented the district consultant has the role of a team leader helping teachers to learn about LFIN and the distinctive assessment and teaching procedures of the programme. For example, each participating teacher conducts individualized assessment interviews with several children. During their project meetings with their district consultant the teachers review and discuss their videotaped interviews. Meetings of this kind prove to be a rich source of professional learning for teachers. LFIN is applied to the results of their assessments of their children's early number knowledge and strategies. This leads to revision of their teaching plans and instructional activities. These revisions take account of the detailed and specific assessment knowledge, and therefore their teaching is more closely tailored to children's current knowledge. In this way CMIT and LFIN have significantly influenced the teaching of early years mathematics across the system.

Glossary

Additive task. A generic label for tasks involving what adults would regard as addition. The label 'additive task' is used to emphasize that children will construe such tasks idiosyncratically, that is differently from each other and from the way adults will construe them.

Advanced counting-by-ones strategies. These strategies are used by a child who has attained at least Stage 3, for example counting-on, counting-down-from and counting-down-to.

Arithmetic Rack. An abacus-like instructional device consisting of two rows of ten beads. In each row the beads appear in two groups of five, that is using two different colours for the beads.

Backward Number Word Sequence (BNWS). A regular sequence of number words backward, typically but not necessarily by ones, for example the BNWS from ten to one, the BNWS from eighty-two to seventy-five, the BNWS by tens from eighty-three.

Combining. An arithmetical strategy involving combining (i.e. adding in a sense) two numbers in the range one to five, without counting, for example 3 and 2, 4 and 4.

Counting-by-ones. Initial or advanced arithmetical strategies which involve counting-by-ones only. Examples of initial counting-by-ones strategies are perceptual and figurative counting, which involve counting-from-one. Examples of advanced counting-by-ones strategies are counting-on, counting-down-from and counting-down-to.

Counting-down-from. A strategy used by children who have attained at least Stage 3 and typically used to solve Removed Items tasks, for example 11 remove 3 – 'eleven, ten, nine – eight!' Also referred to as counting-off-from or counting-back-from.

Counting-down-to. Regarded as the most advanced of the counting-by-ones strategies and used by children who have attained at least Stage 4. Typically used to solve Missing Subtrahend tasks, for example have 11, remove some, and there are eight left – 'eleven, ten, nine – three'. Also referred to as counting-back-to.

Counting-on. An advanced counting-by-ones strategy, indicative of having attained Stage 3, and used to solve additive tasks or Missing Addend tasks involving two hidden collections. Counting-on can be differentiated into counting-up-from for additive tasks and counting-up-to for subtractive tasks. Counting-on is also referred to as counting-up.

Counting-up-from. An advanced counting-by-ones strategy, indicative of having attained Stage 3, and used to solve additive tasks involving two hidden collections, for example seven and five is solved by counting up five from seven.

Counting-up-to. An advanced counting-by-ones strategy, indicative of having attained Stage 3, and used to solve Missing Addend tasks, for example seven and how many make twelve is solved by counting from seven up to twelve, and keeping track of five counts.

Curtailment. Curtailment of a strategy involves modifying the strategy by omitting one or more of the procedures that constitute the strategy. Thus curtailment serves to simplify the strategy and results in a more sophisticated strategy, for example an additive strategy of counting from one is curtailed to a strategy of counting-on by omitting the procedure of counting the first addend from one.

Difference. See Minuend.

Digit. The digits are the ten basic symbols in the modern numeration system, that is '0', '1', ... '9'.

Early Number. A generic label for the number work in the first three years of school and learned by children around four to eight years of age. Also known as 'Early Arithmetic'.

Facile. Used in the sense of have good facility, that is fluent or dexterous, for example a facile counting-on strategy, or facile with the backward number word sequence.

Figurative. The label for Stage 2. Figurative thought involves re-presentation of a sensory-motor experience, that is, a mental replay of a prior experience involving seeing, hearing, touching, etc. Figurative counting may be figural, in which visualized items constitute the material which is counted; motor, in which movements constitute the material which is counted; or verbal, in which number words constitute the material which is counted.

Forward Number Word Sequence (FNWS). A regular sequence of number words forward, typically but not necessarily by ones, for example the FNWS from one to twenty, the FNWS from eighty-one to ninety-three, the FNWS by tens from twenty-four.

Initial counting-by-ones strategies. Strategies characteristic of Stages 1 and 2, for example counting-from-one with visible items (Stage 1) or counting-from-one when items are hidden (Stage 2).

Level. The terms 'Level' and 'Stage' are used in a technical sense. A 'Level' is a point on a continuum, for example Level 3 in knowledge of FNWSs. A 'Stage' is like a plateau. Each new stage is characterized by a qualitative advancement in knowledge, that is a conceptual reorganization of strategies and in the way tasks are construed.

Minuend. In subtraction of standard form, for example $12 - 3 = 9$, 12 is the minuend, 3 is the subtrahend and 9 is the difference. Thus the difference is the answer obtained in subtraction, the subtrahend is the number subtracted and the minuend is the number from which the subtrahend is subtracted.

Missing Addend. A subtractive task posed in the form of addition with one addend missing, for example 12 and how many make 15.

Non-count-by-ones. A class of strategies which involve aspects other than counting-by-ones and which are used to solve additive and subtractive tasks. Part of the strategy may involve counting-by-ones but the solution also involves a more advanced procedure. For example, 6 + 8 is solved by saying 'six and six is twelve – thirteen, fourteen'. These strategies are characteristic of Stage 5.

Number. A number is the idea or concept associated with, for example, how many items in a collection. We distinguish among the number 24 – that is, the concept, the spoken or heard number word 'twenty-four', the numeral '24' and also the read or written number word 'twenty-four'. These distinctions are important in understanding children's early numerical strategies.

Number Word. Number words are names or words for numbers. In most cases in early number, the term 'number word' refers to the spoken and heard names for numbers rather than the read or written names.

Numeral. Numerals are symbols for numbers, for example '5', '27'.

Numeral Identification. Stating the name of a displayed numeral. The term is used similarly to the term 'letter identification' in early literacy. When assessing Numeral Identification, numerals are not displayed in numerical sequence.

Numeral Recognition. Selecting a nominated numeral from a randomly arranged group of numerals.

Numeral sequence. A regularly ordered sequence of numerals, typically but not necessarily a forward sequence by ones, for example the numerals as they appear on a numeral track.

Numeral track. An instructional device consisting of a sequence of numerals and, for each numeral, a hinged lid which may be used to screen or display the numeral.

Numerosity. The numerosity of a collection is the number of items in the collection.

Partitioning. An arithmetical strategy involving partitioning a small number into two parts without counting, typically with both parts in the range 1 to 5, for example partitioning 6 into 5 + 1, 4 + 2, etc.

Partitive. In partitive tasks the dividend and the number of divisors are given and the problem is to work out the quotient. For example, 'How many sweets will each person get if I share 16 sweets among 4 people?'

Perceptual. Involving direct sensory input – usually seeing but may also refer to hearing or feeling. Thus perceptual counting involves counting items seen, heard or felt.

Procedure. See Strategy.

Quinary. This term refers to the use of five as a base in some sense, and typically in conjunction with, rather than instead of, ten as a base. The

Arithmetic Rack may be regarded as a quinary-based instructional device.

Quotitive. In quotitive tasks the divident and the quotient are given and the problem is to work out the number of divisors. For example, 'I have 20 chocolates and I want to give 5 to each person. How many children can I give 5 chocolates to?'

Re-presentation. A re-presentation can be thought of as a mental replay of a prior experience – that is, in reflection, distinct from and separated in time from the experience itself.

Setting. A physical situation used by a teacher in posing numerical tasks, for example collections of counters, Numeral Track, Hundreds Chart, Tens Frame.

Stages. See Levels.

Standard Number Word Sequence (SNWS). The forward sequence of number words from one onward.

Strategy. A generic label for a method by which a child solves a task. A strategy consists of one or more constituent procedures. A procedure is the simplest form of a strategy, that is, a strategy that cannot be described in terms of two or more constituent procedures. For example, on an additive task involving two screened collections a child might use the procedure of counting the first collection from one and then use the procedure of continuing to count by ones, in order to count the second collection.

Subitizing. The immediate, correct assignation of a number word to a small collection of perceptual items.

Subtractive Task. A generic label for tasks involving what adults would regard as subtraction. The label 'subtractive task' is used to emphasize that children will construe such tasks idiosyncratically, that is, differently from each other and from the way adults will construe them.

Subtrahend. See Minuend.

Task. A generic label for problems or questions presented to a child.

Temporal Sequence. A sequence of events that occur sequentially in time, for example sequences of sounds or movements.

Bibliography

Anghileri, J. (1989) An investigation of young children's understanding of multiplication. *Educational Studies in Mathematics*, **20**, 367–85.

Aubrey, C. (1993) An investigation of the mathematical knowledge and competencies which young children bring into school. *British Educational Research Journal*, **19**(1), 27–41.

Bobis, J. (1996) Report of the Evaluation of the Count Me In Too Project. An unpublished report to the NSW Department of Education and Training.

Carpenter, T. P., Ansell, E., Franke, K. L., Fennema, E. and Weisbeck, L. (1993) Models of problem solving: a study of kindergarten children's problem-solving processes. *Journal for Research in Mathematics Education*, **24**, 428–41.

Clark, F. B. and Kamii, C. (1996) Identification of multiplicative thinking in children in grades 1–5. *Journal for Research in Mathematical Education*, **27**, 41–51.

Cobb, P., Boufi, A., McClain, K. and Whitenack, J. (1997a) Reflective discourse and collective reflection. *Journal for Research in Mathematics Education*, **28**, 258–77.

Cobb, P., Gravemeijer, K., Yackel, E., McClain, K. and Whitenack, J. (1997b) Mathematizing and symbolizing: the emergence of chains of signification in one first-grade classroom, in D. Kirshner and J. A. Whitson (eds) *Situated Cognition Theory: Social, Semiotic and Neurological Perspectives* (pp. 151–233) Mahwah, NJ: Lawrence Erlbaum.

Cobb, P., McClain, K., Whitenack, J. and Estes, B. (1995) Supporting young children's development of mathematical power, in A. Richards (ed.) *Proceedings of the Fifteenth Biennial Conference of the Australian Association of Mathematics Teachers* (pp. 1–11) Adelaide, Australia: Australian Association of Mathematics Teachers.

Cobb, P. and Steffe, L. P. (1983) The constructivist researcher as teacher and model builder. *Journal for Research in Mathematics Education*, **14**, 83–94.

Cobb, P. and Wheatley, G. (1988) Children's initial understandings of ten. *Focus on Learning Problems in Mathematics*, **10**(3), 1–26.

Cobb, P., Wood, T. and Yackel, E. (1991) A constructivist approach to second grade mathematics, in E. von. Glasersfeld (ed.) *Radical Constructivism in*

Mathematics Education (pp. 157–76) Dordrecht, The Netherlands: Kluwer.

Cobb, P., Wood, T. and Yackel, E. (1992) Interaction and learning in classroom situations. *Educational Studies in Mathematics,* 23, 99–122.

Cockcroft, W. H. (1982) (The Cockcroft Report) *Mathematics Counts: Report of the Committee of Inquiry into the Teaching of Mathematics in Schools.* London: HMSO.

Confrey, J. (1994) Splitting, similarity, and rate of change: a new approach to multiplication and exponential functions, in G. Harel and J. Confrey (eds) *The Development of Multiplicative Reasoning in the Learning of Mathematics* (pp. 291–330) Albany, NY: State University of New York Press.

Denvir, B. and Brown, M. (1986a) Understanding of number concepts in low attaining 7–9 year olds: Part 1. Development of descriptive framework and diagnostic instrument. *Educational Studies in Mathematics,* 17, 15–36.

Denvir, B. and Brown, M. (1986b) Understanding of number concepts in low attaining 7–9 year olds: Part II. The teaching studies. *Educational Studies in Mathematics,* 17, 143–64.

DfEE (1999a) *Framework for Teaching Mathematics from Reception to Year 6.* Cambridge: Cambridge University Press.

DfEE (1999b) *National Numeracy Strategy: Mathematical Vocabulary.* London: DfEE.

Glasersfeld, E. von (1982) Subitizing: the role of figural patterns in the development of numerical concepts. *Archives de Psychologie,* 50, 191–218.

Glasersfeld, E. von and Kelley, M. (1982) On the concepts of period, phase, stage and level. *Human Development,* 25, 152–60.

Gravemeijer, K. P. E. (1994) *Developing Realistic Mathematics Education.* Utrecht, The Netherlands: CD-B Press.

Hunting, R. P., Davis, G. and Pearn, C. (1996) Engaging whole-number knowledge for rational-number learning using a computer-based tool. *Journal for Research in Mathematics Education,* 27, 354–79.

Kouba, V. L. (1989) Children's solution strategies for equivalent set multiplication and division word problems. *Journal for Research in Mathematics Education,* 20, 147–58.

Mulligan, J. T. (1998) A research-based framework for assessing early multiplication and division, in C. Kanes, M. Goos and E. Warren (eds) *Proceedings of the 21st Annual Conference of the Mathematics Education Research Group of Australasia* (Vol. 2, pp. 404–11). Brisbane: Griffith University.

Mulligan, J. T. and Mitchelmore, M. C. (1997) Young children's intuitive models of multiplication and division. *Journal for Research in Mathematics Education,* 28, 309–30.

National Council for Teachers of Mathematics (NCTM). *Principles and Standards for School Mathematics: Discussion Draft, October 1998.*

Reston, VA: NCTM.

National Numeracy Project (1999) *Numeracy Lessons*. Reading: National Centre for Numeracy.

NSW Department of Education and Training (1998) *Count Me In Too: A Professional Development Package*. Sydney: NSWDET.

Numeracy = Everyone's Business (1997) Report of the Numeracy Education Strategy Development Conference. Adelaide: Australian Association of Mathematics Teachers.

QCA (1999a) *Standards in Mathematics: exemplification of Key Learning Objectives from Reception to Year 6*. London: QCA.

QCA (1999b) *The National Numeracy Strategy: Teaching Mental Calculation Strategies; Guidance for Teachers at Key Stages 1 and 2*. London: QCA.

Smith, J. P. (1996) Efficacy and teaching mathematics by telling: a challenge for reform. *Journal for Research in Mathematics Education*, 27, 387–402.

Steffe, L. P. (1992a) Learning stages in the construction of the number sequence, in J. Bideaud, C. Meljac and J. Fischer (eds) *Pathways to Number: Children's Developing Numerical Abilities* (pp. 83–88) Hillsdale, NJ: Lawrence Erlbaum.

Steffe, L. P. (1992b) Schemes of action and operation involving composite units. *Learning and Individual Differences*, 4, 259–309.

Steffe, L. P. (1994) Children's multiplying schemes, in G. Harel and J. Confrey (eds) *The Development of Multiplicative Reasoning in the Learning of Mathematics* (pp. 3–41) Albany, NY: State University of New York Press.

Steffe, L. P. and Cobb, P. (with E. von Glasersfeld) (1988) *Construction of Arithmetic Meanings and Strategies*. New York: Springer-Verlag.

Steffe, L. P., von Glasersfeld, E., Richards, J. and Cobb, P. (1983) *Children's Counting Types: Philosophy, Theory and Application*. New York: Praeger.

Wright, R. J. (1989) Numerical development in the kindergarten year: a teaching experiment. Doctoral Dissertation, University of Georgia.

Wright, R. J. (1991a) An application of the epistemology of radical constructivism to the study of learning. *Australian Educational Researcher*, 18(1), 75–95.

Wright, R. J. (1991b) What number knowledge is possessed by children entering the kindergarten year of school? *Mathematics Education Research Journal*, 3(1), 1–16.

Wright, R. J. (1994) A study of the numerical development of 5-year-olds and 6-year-olds. *Educational Studies in Mathematics*, 26, 25–44.

Wright, R. J. (1996) Problem-centred mathematics in the first year of school, in J. Mulligan and M. Mitchelmore (eds) *Children's Number Learning: A Research Monograph of the Mathematics Education Research Group of Australasia* (pp. 35–54) Adelaide: AAMT.

Wright, R. J. (1999) Professional development in recovery education, in L. P. Steffe and P. W. Thompson (eds) *Radical Constructivism in Action:*

Building on the Pioneering Work of Ernst von Glasersfeld. London: Falmer.

Wright, R. J., Cowper, M., Stafford, A., Stanger, G. and Stewart, R. (1994) The Maths Recovery Project: a progress report, in G. Bell, R. Wright, N. Leeson and J. Geake (eds) *Proceedings of the Seventeenth Annual Conference of the Mathematics Education Research Group of Australasia* (Vol. 2, pp. 709–16). Lismore, NSW, Australia: Southern Cross University.

Wright, R. J., Stanger, G., Cowper, M. and Dyson, R. (1996) First-graders' progress in an experimental mathematics recovery program, in J. Mulligan and M. Mitchelmore (eds) *Children's Number Learning: A Research Monograph of the Mathematics Education Research Group of Australasia* (pp. 55–72) Adelaide: AAMT.

Wright, R. J., Stewart, R., Stafford, A. and Cain, R. (1998) Assessing and documenting student knowledge and progress in early mathematics, in S. B. Berenson, K. R. Dawkins, M. Blanton, W. N. Coulombe, J. Kolb, K. Norwood and L. Stiff (eds) *Proceedings of the Twentieth Annual Meeting of the North American Chapter of the International Group for the Psychology of Mathematics Education* (Vol. 1, pp. 211–16). Columbus, OH: ERIC Clearinghouse for Science, Mathematics and Environmental Education.

Yackel, E., Cobb, P. and Wood, T. (1991) Small group interactions as a source of learning opportunities in second grade mathematics. *Journal for Research in Mathematics Education*, 22, 390–408.

Young-Loveridge, J. (1989) The development of children's number concepts: the first year of school. *New Zealand Journal of Educational Studies*, 24(1), 47–64.

Young-Loveridge, J. (1991) *The Development of Children's Number Concepts from Ages Five to Nine, Volumes 1 and 2*. Hamilton, NZ: University of Waikato.

Index